LOST & FOUND

SENLUX

NOV 2016

Books by Sarah Jakes

Colliding With Destiny
Lost & Found
Dear Mary

SARAH JAKES

LOST & FOUND

Finding HOPE *in the Detours of Life*

BETHANY HOUSE PUBLISHERS

a division of Baker Publishing Group
Minneapolis, Minnesota

Published by Bethany House Publishers
11400 Hampshire Avenue South
Bloomington, Minnesota 55438
www.bethanyhouse.com

Bethany House Publishers is a division of
Baker Publishing Group, Grand Rapids, Michigan

Paperback edition published 2015
ISBN 978-0-7642-1699-2

Printed in the United States of America

The Library of Congress has cataloged the hardcover edition as follows:
Jakes, Sarah.
    Lost and found : finding hope in the detours of life / Sarah Jakes ; foreword by T.D. Jakes.
        pages cm
    Summary: "An inspiring personal account of overcoming past mistakes and finding faith and purpose again from a young woman who was pregnant at fourteen, then married and divorced in her twenties"— Provided by publisher.
    ISBN 978-0-7642-1209-3 (cloth : alk. paper) — ISBN 978-0-7642-1241-3 (international trade paper : alk. paper) 1. Jakes, Sarah. 2. African American Pentecostals—Biography. 3. African American women—Religious life. I. Title.
BX8762.5.Z8J33 2014
289.9′409—dc23   2013039788
                                                                                              [B]

Cover design by Peter Gloege | LOOK Design Studio
Front cover photography by Brian Braun
Back cover photography by Will Sterling

Author is represented by Dupree/Miller & Associates

16 17 18 19 20 21 22   8 7 6 5 4 3 2

Because of family I'll never be able to fully thank, friends that could never be replaced, and a blog that encouraged more people than I'll ever get the chance to hug . . .

For the tears I cried and the ones I held on the inside. For the truth I wanted to erase and lies I thought I had to tell.

Then there are the two hearts that grew inside of me that protected me from dangers I'll never know.

The insecurities I thought I could never love and the past I tried to escape. Because I believe all things, even our missteps, work together for the good of those who love Him.

I gave Him my pain.
I gave Him my shame.
And He gave me the grace to heal.

Contents

Foreword

I NEVER THOUGHT as I rushed down the hall to the delivery room to visit my newly born daughter that the day would eventually come when I would be writing a foreword preparing your heart for one of the most riveting experiences of her life and my own. At that time I hadn't been established as a writer myself, so I guess it was totally beyond my imagination that a day like this would come. Who would've thought that this little bundle of purity and protoplasm would bud and blossom through thorns and thistles and ultimately evolve to the degree that she has indeed been transformed.

I came into the hospital room; I had not long to refresh myself after her mother's labor. Neither my wife nor I had caught even a minimal amount of sleep. So I was back at the hospital, dressed in a black suit and a black clergy shirt as it was Sunday morning, and I had in my hands a brand-new red and white ruffled dress for the baby to come home in later. She was the newest member to the Jakes clan. I also had in my other hand a worn Bible whose pages promised the Savior would never leave me nor forsake me. He didn't leave me.

But I would come to learn that His promise wasn't to my wife and me alone but would also extend to our seed!

Later I would lift her up into my arms and feel her fragile little body fit neatly in my hand, almost like the Bible I had when I arrived. Little Sarah, laying in white sheets, cooing from her crib, was almost as red-faced as the dress I had bought her. She looked up at me with walnut-shaped eyes that were almost as dark as a fine piece of onyx. She smiled a coy smile that would later be the catalyst from which I would become solidly and sometimes completely wrapped around her little finger. Some of you will remember I wrote the book *Daddy Loves His Girls*. I guess it is the way that many fathers experience waves of that protective love in the presence of their daughters. Anyway, her toothless grin radiated sunshine from her bed, and I can still remember the sweet scent of fresh baby oil and powder coming from her body. She was simply amazing!

What a surprise she was to us all. Her older sister was less than a year her senior. I had already been juggling twin boys, and now two girls, in my arms simultaneously. I was a struggling pastor who had lost his job at a chemical plant and was fighting to feed my family between feeding a small flock of church members in a rural area when she was born. At that moment I was uncertain that I would ever be able to adequately feed either the church or the children the way I desired. But I purposed in my heart to give both my best! Still, none of those bleak realities diminished the dimples on her cheeks or the effervescence of her radiant eyes as she stared at me from the crib.

Given the turbulence of the times in which she was born to us, I should've known that this was the beginning of an adventure as wild as an Indy 500 race car on an oil spill! I can assure you of one thing, there was seldom a dull moment back then. So when Sarah tells her story, all I can say to you is fasten your seat belts; you are in for a real ride!

Given our meager fare, and my concern with girding, guarding, and guiding my family, I was more preoccupied with provisions than purpose. This is a common proclivity among men. I looked at her and thought to myself, *How am I going to feed another mouth?* Still, as I gazed at her somehow she distracted me from my focus on my responsibilities, and I found myself smiling at her little face.

For a moment I was wondering how this new arrival would affect our lives, and not just how she would add to our already strained budget. To all of this she just looked at me, opened her mouth wide, and yawned! She was something else. She was totally oblivious to the world's economy, my layoff from the job, or anything else. It was nap time to her. That was all that mattered, and she just dozed off, fast asleep in my arms, leaving me to figure the rest out!

These were the early years of our lives. It was the beginning of a saga that would often be filled with uncontrollable laughter, as all my children have a real sense of humor. And at other moments we had an unspeakable concern and anguish as we steered all five children through the turbulence of adolescence. And if that weren't enough to make your green eyes blue, we would be destined to figure it out while adjusting to living in the public's glaring eye. We had gone from a simple rural life in a small town to life in the very fast lane of a cosmopolitan city. It was a world as foreign to us as a sky loft apartment on the planet Mars! But I guess it doesn't matter the backdrop, life is always an adventure from which only the strong survive. All of us have a story to tell. But not all of us survive to tell what happened and how we triumphed over the many tragedies that happened along the way.

The path we were to travel was as curvaceous as the West Virginia roads where Sarah made her entry into this world. Even back then we had some battles, but none of those challenges prepared us for the category-five storms that hit us when we loaded up the truck, like the Beverly Hillbillies, and headed to the bright lights and bustling highways of Dallas. In a few short years we would lose both my wife's mother and my own. Illness would strike my wife multiple times and back pain would drive me to surgery.

I was too young myself to understand that all storms have an expiration date. I didn't know that tough times are a part of life. That there is an end to tears and that they do dry up with faith and prayer. Little did I know that after deep pain and heartburn beyond belief that wisdom falls like the morning dew and that we would collectively become eyewitnesses to the transformation of a human soul from the best front-row seats imaginable. These are the seats you sit in when the drama you see on television and read about in the papers is now being acted out in your house!

I guess I should at least warn you. Do not expect a Sunday school storybook filled with Christian colloquialisms and religious rhetoric. Nor are you about to read a stereotypical memoir of young ladies' or little girls' experiences while growing up. Instead you will see the perspective of one little girl whose childhood was nearly stolen by "grown woman" experiences. But today she has become a tool fit for the Master's use.

I will leave you now for Sarah to share the life lessons that have come our way. I pray that it ministers to you as it did to me. And I pray that your thirst is quenched at the living well of Christ's eternal spring, as He deserves the glory for this book and the outcome of this story. It is to that eternal fountain that both my daughter and I invite you to come. Come and drink from the place where lost souls are found and lost passion is reborn. This is the gushing geyser of truth that may very well ignite your dreams to flourish as you encounter what God does with a child whose parents' prayers are answered in her response to His sovereign call. No matter how bleak the night, hold on. Joy really does come in the morning. For a moment we almost lost her to the dark night. But like the father of the prodigal son, her mother and I are thrilled to see her come back down the road. My daughter was indeed lost and found!

Bishop T.D. Jakes

Introduction

Getting Lost

AS THE MOTHER of two elementary-age kids, I've learned that over the course of a school year a lot of things go missing. A backpack, water bottle, jacket, hat—you name it—simply doesn't make it home after school one day. My casual questions about the location of a particular missing item are usually met with a blank stare by my son or daughter.

The first few times, this was very frustrating. It felt like I cared more about a *Dora the Explorer* lunch box than my daughter did. Or that I would miss my son's basketball more than he would. But then I became acquainted with the secret that almost all parents learn to utilize in recovering half their child's possessions: the lost-and-found shelf at school.

Even if the recovered items are small or seemingly trivial, I still love the feeling of finding something that was lost. Who hasn't left their car keys in a jacket pocket or forgotten their phone in a waiting room and felt the relief and gratitude for finding it—then made the mental note not to let it happen again?

So much of our lives revolves around the pain of what we've lost. And the joy of what we've found.

From time to time, we all lose things. Yet some things we aren't always able to locate and recover. Lost time is certainly one of these. And everyone who knows me will testify that time management is one of the areas of my life where I need the most improvement. No matter how hard I try to be on time, it rarely happens.

In the hours before I'm scheduled to be at an appointment, time ticks by so slowly. Then inevitably something comes up and it seems like someone has pressed fast-forward on my life. Suddenly I'm racing around my bedroom to get ready, hoping I won't be embarrassingly late. A quick look in the mirror and I'm off to the car.

Then once behind the wheel it hits me: I don't really know where I'm going. But once I've mapped out the best route to reach my destination and am on the road, I finally relax. I know I'm going to be a little late, but it won't be too bad, maybe by just a minute or two. I turn to my favorite radio station, humming the words to my favorite tune. As soon as my heart reaches a steady pace, however, the cars in front of me begin braking. One by one the red lights appear, signaling my biggest fear.

I'm going to be very, utterly, embarrassingly late.

The traffic is at a standstill for as far as the eye can see. My exit is just a couple exits up from where I am, though, so I start veering off the highway. Surely I can find a side street that runs parallel with the highway to help me reach my exit. Turn after turn, decision after decision, I end up more lost and even later than I would have been had I just stayed on the highway stuck in traffic.

I hate it. I hate feeling like maybe I wouldn't be so late if I had not started doing the laundry or had just waited to paint my toes. I wouldn't be so far behind had I not walked the dog and washed the car. If only I hadn't become impatient and tried to find an alternate route. If only I had planned to be early for once.

Sometimes I find myself wondering just how much I have lost in life because of the moments when I tried to find my own way and ended up more lost than ever. What if I had waited to fall in love? Or if I had just finished that course, would I have graduated by now? I wonder who I could have been had I never taken a wrong turn on my life's journey. Without all those wrong turns and unexpected delays, who would I have become?

As if these questions aren't enough, I also feel taunted by the idea that I'm late. Can you relate? The later it seems we'll be, the less important the destination becomes. We think to ourselves, "I can't fix my life now—I'd have to start all over"; "I can't dare to love again—it's too late"; "I made a wrong choice, and now I'd rather stay here than try again." How often do we become lost in the maze of our own mistakes? How stubborn have we become that we refuse to ask for directions or assistance along the way?

Too often, life has a way of making us believe that each wrong turn means we'll never end up at our divinely appointed destination. But that's not true. We must take a moment and stop our questioning and what-ifs to realize that time, like life, isn't about how much we have; it's about what we do with it.

> *Time, like life, isn't about how much we have; it's about what we do with it.*

It's a funny thing, feeling lost. It makes you feel like you're out of control. Being lost is most frustrating when you know you have an appointment to keep. When you get lost on a casual day, it becomes an adventure, an unexpected few moments to relax with some quiet time away from others.

Driving around and getting lost can become an exhilarating escape when you don't feel like other people are watching the clock and wondering where you are. The burdens of the day, weighing on you so heavily that you'd rather be in a car taking the long way home than to admit that your reality is worse than your fantasy, slip away with your favorite song on the radio and the sun warming your face.

Sometimes you find yourself when you get lost.

———

If you had told me the girl who got pregnant at thirteen and felt like the black sheep child of America's favorite preacher would now be a twenty-five-year-old single mom, divorcée, author, motivational speaker, TV personality, ministry director, and senior editor, I never would have believed you. But knowing it's true, that I'm all these things and so much more now, I'd say the only way to get your bearings and find yourself is to trust that you were never really lost. Amid all your twists and turns, perhaps you simply haven't discovered the right direction yet.

God loves the lost. And He loves to help us find our way when we turn to Him and ask directions. Jesus talked a lot about lost things. About a poor woman who lost her only coin and then swept every inch of her house until she found it. About a compassionate shepherd who noticed that one of his sheep had strayed from the other ninety-nine and needed to be rescued. About a loving daddy who let his rebellious son do his own thing before he came crawling back home to his dad's open arms.

Often we think about our salvation experience as one of being lost before we are found. And this is true. But I also think that even though we may be found, sooner or later we'll turn down a side street looking for a shortcut, finding ourselves lost again. Just because our salvation is intact doesn't mean we always know where we're going.

No matter how lost you feel, it's not too late.

You can still get to where God destined you to go.

He's waiting to find you no matter how often you lose your way.

My life now is everything I ever needed, but nothing I ever wanted. Growing up, I dreamed of doing things the "right" way. So I made decisions to create my vision of what I thought would perfect my image. After the unraveling of each of those attempts, I found myself lost—down-to-my-knees, tears-on-my-face, scars-on-my-heart *lost*. I came to understand the only way I could be found was to admit I was lost. Because I realized that when princesses don't follow directions, they can't inherit the palaces that their Father the King has waiting for them.

We can't find our way home unless we admit we're lost.

My life now is everything I ever needed, but nothing I ever wanted.

In the pages that follow, I want to share my story with you. And yes, I realize that you may wonder what I, having lived only a quarter century, could possibly have to say to fill up an entire book. But I think if you'll share my journey, somewhere along the way you will recognize yourself and your own experiences of being lost and found. And my hope is that whatever grace I've tasted and whatever wisdom I've gathered can now be given to you. My story is not always pretty, but I think you'll agree that parts of it are beautiful. The parts where God finds me and reminds me who I am. The moments when He sees me as His daughter on a divine collision course with my destiny.

The same way He sees you.

1

Growing Up Jakes

OVER THIRTY YEARS ago my parents, T.D. and Serita Jakes, started a ministry that catapulted our lives onto a platform none of us could have ever imagined. In 2001, *Time* featured my father on the cover and labeled him "The Next Billy Graham." For many years now, our church, The Potter's House in Dallas, Texas, has remained one of the fastest-growing churches in the nation. With over thirty-five thousand members and four locations, the church has grown from fifty families to thousands of families within sixteen years.

My parents have also written bestselling books, spoken before crowds larger than the population of our hometown, and produced award-winning plays and movies. My father has won Grammy Awards and has been honored by the NAACP. Oprah has dined at our house, and Aretha Franklin has performed for my dad's ministry. My parents have traveled the world, from Africa to Arkansas to Australia, preaching and empowering people with a message of hope. I've been privileged to experience most of these milestones with them.

But it all started slowly and quietly, at least for me, before taking on a life of its own. I spent the first eight years of my life in Charleston, West Virginia. It's certainly not New York, Los Angeles, Chicago, or Dallas, but it was the first and only version of a "city" I knew. Driving a few minutes in any direction from Charleston would take you into neighborhoods where people would greet you like family and offer to assist you with directions. It was a city with a small-town feel.

We hardly ever went anywhere in our town where my parents didn't see someone they knew "way back when." There are very few strangers in West Virginia. To this day, if my father or mother learns someone they've met is from their native state, they ask questions about whom they're related to. Whether we were in a restaurant or attending a meeting, they would find two or three degrees of separation between them and their fellow West Virginian.

Everyone in school knew who we were, the Jakes kids, but our classmates never asked many questions about our family or the work they did. Their parents probably knew ours or they knew someone else who knew us. We weren't famous or anything, just familiar. There was something comfortably secure about being known—again, that sense of being in a small-town community that appreciated its own. I felt safe.

My childhood in Charleston wasn't like living in Mayberry, but it was a special time. I remember church trips with sweet potato pies and deviled eggs, barbecued chicken and banana pudding. The men and women of our church became aunts and uncles. They would tell our parents if they caught us kids misbehaving or give us our favorite candy when they saw us round the corner. When we ran through the church between services, someone would grab us and tell us to slow down. No one considered this overstepping a boundary. They were just the village that was helping to raise us.

My sister, Cora, is only eleven months and twenty-nine days older than I am. Her birthday is July 19, mine is July 17. I suspect we figured out the math for purely selfish reasons: I wanted to prove that she really wasn't that much older than I, and she wanted to assure me that even if it was a minute, older is older.

We were in the same grade and class for most of our lives. While we would sometimes get mad and argue like sisters do, we were also a formidable team together. You see, siblings are usually either adversaries or partners in crime. Whether dialing 9-1-1 on the alarm system when playing house or swinging on doors as budding gymnasts, Cora and I managed to have quite a bit of fun. Unfortunately, that fun almost always ended in trouble. You might think we would've learned our lesson after a few times, but to this day we can't resist a good adventure.

Interestingly enough, my parents were hardly ever amused by our shenanigans. One time my sister and I grew tired of keeping one another busy with our homemade games and decided to go outside to play. After running around the yard awhile, I convinced Cora that we should drive our parents' car. Of course, I meant we should pretend to drive, but as we sat in the car, the idea of actually driving seemed way more exciting.

The next thing I knew, my sister handed me the keys. I turned them the same way I had observed my mother and father doing it hundreds of times before. When I shifted into gear, we immediately rolled down the hill, taking out a few trash cans and a mailbox or two along our street. Thankfully, that incident didn't result in any other casualties. Turns out that rolling down the hill in our parents'

Lincoln wasn't what we should have been afraid of. The true fear should have been of their reaction!

Needless to say, Cora and I got in trouble. At the time we must have felt really misunderstood about the entire situation, because we concocted a plan. Funny how one mistake sometimes leads to another. Our plan for revenge was inspired by one of our favorite movies at the time, *Mrs. Doubtfire*.

Released in 1993, the film revolves around a married couple who decide to separate. In an effort to spend more time with his children, the father, portrayed by Robin Williams, secures a job as his children's nanny by dressing as a much older woman. In full regalia, his character transforms from a fun-loving, somewhat reckless dad into a frumpy, wise, and wisecracking caretaker. With his alter ego's help, he soon finds the perfect balance of responsibility and excitement.

Finding the balance was not easy, though. In one of the scenes, he has to punish his children and forces them to clean the entire house from top to bottom while he ("she") sits on the couch with a glass of lemonade and a newspaper. This scene inspired Cora and me in the aftermath of our little joyride.

We decided that we would tell our teacher that our mother was abusing us in the same way Mrs. Doubtfire punished the children in our favorite film. Yes, our mother was making us use harsh chemicals and do backbreaking work while she sat on the couch enjoying lemonade and watching television. In hindsight, I'm not exactly sure what we thought would happen by telling that story on our mom, but somehow we were sure we'd be vindicated. Thankfully, West Virginia was the kind of place where it wasn't difficult to investigate the credibility of such a claim.

Our teacher did not believe us. She knew too well our family and our parents' ministry. Truth be told, she may have even been distantly related to us.

Needless to say, she destroyed our foolproof plan and had a good laugh with our mother about such a crazy scheme. We, on the other hand, found ourselves in even deeper trouble.

I laugh about it now and appreciate the way this incident reminds me of a simpler, more innocent time. This was the beauty of West Virginia. It didn't take a lot of work to find the heart and intentions of the people you interacted with each and every day. They were good people.

My father once said that family is love's gymnasium. I instantly knew it was true. We learn how differently people show their love in their relationships with family. Since we're so close in age, my sister and I have always been a pair who shared a special bond. People always thought she and I were the twins in our family. But our brothers Jamar and Jermaine are the actual twins. Eight years our senior, they hardly ever ran in the same circles as Cora and I or our younger brother, Dexter. But no matter the differences in our ages, through the ups and downs of one another's lives, all five of us learned to hold on to one another.

When I was a child, Jamar, older than Jermaine by twenty-eight minutes, represented everything I thought an adult was supposed to be. He was never visibly shaken, rarely seemed out of control, and always knew the right thing to do. If there was an emergency—say, Cora and I locked ourselves out of the house—we knew to call Jamar. He could get us out of trouble and back to Mom and Dad without a problem.

> *We learn how differently people show their love in their relationships with family.*

Those characteristics were also why we thought he was mean. He was always so serious and responsible, so protective over us. At the time, we thought he didn't want us to have any fun. As we matured, we learned he was trying to save us from trouble. We interpret things so differently after the scars teach us. We could have been spared many time-outs, spankings, and other troubles had we just listened to Jamar.

For Jamar, love means having your back, especially when you don't have it yourself. He can't bear to watch idly as someone he loves struggles. And while he often shies away from the stage our life brings, it's not because he's without talent. He could easily set the world on fire with the display of just one of his gifts. He's loyal to the cause and courageously resists the pressure to evolve before his own timing.

When we were looking for bedtime stories, gut-busting jokes, or a safe place from the monsters beneath our bed, we went to Jermaine. His love is infectious. A beautiful writer, Maine, as we call him, has always been sensitive to the power of words as well as silence. He's careful with what he says and never hesitates to apologize if he's offended anyone. His heart is constantly in the right place, probably on his sleeve unless he's already given you the shirt off his back.

Jermaine, much like my mother, has always been sensitive to the feelings of others. There's this thing about growing up in a large family: When you get in trouble, everyone in the house knows it. What's so bad about that? Well, all of those family members have friends, and then their friends know you're in trouble. Guess what makes it better? Those friends go to your church and have friends whom they tell, too. By the time your news has traveled all around home, church, and school, you're in need of just one friend. That was Jermaine. I suspect that he inherited a gene from our mom that made him naturally want to hug us after we got in trouble.

I was the baby of my family for six years, one of the best times in my life. Then there was Hawaii. My youngest brother, Dexter, arrived and stole my spotlight. After I got over the no-longer-the-baby blues, Dexter became my ally. Cora and I didn't always get along, you see. She often wanted to watch *Saved by the Bell*, while I wanted to watch *The Fresh Prince of Bel-Air*. Whenever she and I argued about such life-changing decisions, I brought in Dexter to break the tie. Even though he was my baby brother, I never shooed him away or made him feel like his thoughts weren't valuable. I tried to be the perfect combination of what I loved most about Jamar and Jermaine.

Dexter, quickly too tall to be called my little brother, has always found a safe place talking to me. I take my role as his big sister very seriously. I spent many years looking out for him. Whether it was helping him with his homework or going on McDonald's runs, I made sure he knew that, even though he didn't have a sibling close in age, it didn't mean he didn't have a sibling close. The more he matured, the more he reciprocated in our relationship. He's fiercely protective of his big sister. There's hardly anything more in life that I want than for him to succeed.

Moving to Dallas changed many things about our family, but the core of our values and relationships remained centered on our love for one another. And we would need those bonds because we were all about to be tested.

"Girls," my father said as he looked at Cora and me. We were about eight and nine at the time. "Your mother and I have something exciting to share with you." They asked us to stop playing and come and sit with them. We wondered what we'd done now, because we knew something was up.

Our mother sat beside us on the brown sofa in our living room, suppressing a smile. Something like change was in the air, the feeling we would have at Christmas that something wonderful was about to happen, a gift about to be given. My thoughts raced through possibilities: Were we getting a puppy? Or moving to a new house? Or going to have another brother or sister? Or . . . ?

"We believe the Lord is calling us to move the church to Dallas," my father said, managing to sound both enthusiastic and calm at the same time. "So we will be moving there soon."

"That's in Texas," our mother added, finally allowing her smile to bloom.

Cora and I looked at each other with bulging eyes and childish grins. We had no idea what it meant to move to Dallas, That's-in-Texas, but it sure sounded exciting. Cowboys and horses and open prairies and all the Wild West stuff we had only seen on TV galloped through my mind.

Our parents went on to explain that a number of other families from the church, about fifty, would be moving with us. I probably couldn't have even pointed out Dallas on a map, but we were all so excited. Sure enough, we would get to see actual cowboys with boots and hats. Texas might as well have been a foreign country. Yes, our move would be an adventure, just not one my young mind could fully comprehend.

Always the planner and provider, our father went before us to find a home. While we were sad to leave Charleston, there was something that just felt right about moving to Dallas. When we finally boarded the plane to leave West Virginia, Cora and I were thinking of what our new room would look like and how many laps we could run through the new church before tiring out.

Within minutes of being in Texas air, we knew everything would be different. Their side roads looked like major highways compared with where we were from. And Texas highways looked like giant jigsaw puzzles, with bridges and overpasses spanning as far as the eye could see. People seemed to be everywhere, buzzing here and there, from suburb to suburb—each one like a small city. Strip malls were everywhere, along with lots of construction. Where were all the cowboys?

To say there was some culture shock is putting it mildly. The year we moved to Dallas, 1996, the state of West Virginia had a population of 1.8 million. Texas's population was 19 million. At that time there were over 1,400 reported murders in Texas—more than twenty times West Virginia's 69 cases. Certainly Texas is a much larger state than West Virginia, but having spent our parents' entire pastorate in our hometown, how could we have known the issues would be so drastically different from our norm?

Once we spent a few days getting settled and adjusting to a Texas summer (heat that took my breath away), our first Sunday rolled around. It would be our first time introducing new local members to our preexisting church family. It would be the first time our family would be interacting with new people in a long time. Even as a child, I could sense that this moment was incredibly important.

When that Sunday arrived, my siblings and I were swarmed by anxious children wanting to meet us, their new church family. Literally hundreds of children came running toward us, and instantly we knew that we were far from Charleston. They were so warm and friendly, but it was still a little overwhelming. I think people just wanted to know who we were, what we looked like, what type of personalities and funny accents we had brought with us from West Virginia.

The feeling was mutual, though, because we wanted to get to know them. We were dying to know what happened to the cowboys, horses, and tumbleweeds. Instantly, we had all of these friends who just wanted to get to know more about us and our family. It seemed quite harmless at that age. We weren't concerned with determining people's intentions. It never dawned on us that people might not care about who we were on the inside and instead be more concerned with how successful we appeared and how they could position themselves close to us.

Something was beginning to shift—in me, in our family, in the ministry—although at the time I wasn't sure what it was. Later that evening when we sat down for dinner, I overheard my parents recapping their first Sunday at The Potter's House. Fifteen hundred people joined the church that day.

Most of our new church family had already been following the ministry from their homes. Many had tuned in to see this dynamic young minister, T.D. Jakes, preaching at a conference called Azusa, a contemporary spiritual gathering which honored the Azusa Street Revival that had begun in Los Angeles around 1906. From speaking at Azusa, my father soon became a mainstay on the Trinity Broadcasting Network (TBN). He also started publishing books that became bestsellers.

I wish there was one distinct moment when I could tell you the church went from fifteen hundred to over thirty-six thousand, but from my young eyes all of it was so big. Since an early age, I've never understood why some people criticized the size of our church. Were we supposed to put a limit on how many souls could be saved? I used to laugh at the idea of putting up a Closed sign on the main entrance to the sanctuary. I wonder what critics would have thought about that! Were we supposed to turn the people away?

Our greatest challenge in starting the church was not its size. I'm convinced it had much more to do with maintaining tradition in an ever-evolving world. Moving to Texas was so much bigger than starting a church. My father, and a few others like him, had unprecedented access to a world often shunned and called secular. But instead of supporting this progression, many critiqued it. How do we show the world the power of God's love when we, as Christians, fail so often to show love to one another?

I grew up hearing people call my father a thief, a liar, and a cheater. Regardless of how many times his books landed on the *New York Times* bestseller lists or how many speaking engagements he booked each year or, later, how many films he produced, critics popped up to insist that our groceries were purchased with money from the church offering plates.

It was so frustrating. We grew up with our father sitting in the family room asking us about our day, so tired from working that he'd fall asleep before we could finish answering. As a family we've sat in waiting rooms for back surgeries and knee surgeries necessitated by our parents' bearing the weight of being human and the demands of being called, caring for others before themselves. I remember my father flying out of town on Christmas Day so that he could preach at a revival on December 26. We learned the beauty in quality, not quantity, so that lives could literally be saved by a word from God. How could you let a birthday cake compete with that?

How do we show the world the power of God's love when we, as Christians, fail so often to show love to one another?

Earlier in their lives, after they had just married but before the ministry began to bloom, my father was digging ditches to support my mom and older brothers. Three children later, it was no surprise that he had to work nonstop to support his family. I figured if he had to be gone, at least it was helping someone else to become better.

We didn't get that many walks in the park. It wasn't very often Dad helped us with our homework. Which probably turned out to be a good thing, in hindsight. We cherished our time with him more and became fiercely protective. We shared our father's voice with millions, but we were content holding his heart. That intense desire to protect his heart made us more than angry at the criticism—I think it hurt us more than him sometimes.

I constantly questioned our overall goal in Christianity. Much larger than the tradition of church, I wondered who was willing to truly carry out the Great Commission. How can we reach those people we aren't even willing to acknowledge? The homeless, the shift workers, the children on the street, the single mothers, the addicts and ex-cons, the lonely old people, the widows and orphans. How can we save someone if we don't hear his or her cries for help?

Do we have to constantly infect the wounds of others by picking at their weaknesses?

Are we all not just flesh, bones, hearts, and spirits searching for a purpose greater than ourselves? We may not always get it right, but do we have to constantly infect the wounds of others by picking at their weaknesses? I have no heaven or hell to put anyone in. I just have this belief that God didn't call me to police His kingdom. How can we be on the same team, yet allow our differences to make us competition? How can we ever show the power of God to heal if we insist on constantly bruising one another? I've seen so many people lose their way in ministry because they were unwilling to pretend to have it all together. How can we represent a God who loved us enough He died for our sins, yet undermine His sacrifice by further crucifying those who need Him?

We've all watched in shock as people we admire have their darkest struggles and secrets exposed. Yet instead of admitting that we, too, have a weakness that required God's touch, we leave people in their misery.

I was never comfortable with the isolation of those whose sin revealed their humanity. I would rather be an outcast in a room of hypocrites. Tradition thinks that rebellion is the disease; I know now it's the symptom. By definition a rebel is someone unconventional. I didn't feel like the "ordinary" church girl, so I refused to conform to a role that wasn't genuine for me. I wonder how different things would be if we gave people the room to be who God created them to be and not what we want or need.

One of my favorite stories in the Bible is about the shepherd who leaves the ninety-nine and goes back for the one lost sheep. I have been that lost sheep. In fact, I probably will be again before my time on this earth is done, but I am sure of one thing. My biggest fear wasn't that I wouldn't survive being lost; it was that I was alone. The moment I found God, I wasn't where I was supposed to be, but He knew that. I wonder what was keeping me from Him. I was the one lost, and I knew God had the way out, yet I was still afraid. It's amazing how the opinions of the ninety-nine keep the one from coming back. I was afraid I'd be judged. My father's ministry—and my Father's ministry—was never meant for the ones who knew their place. It was for the ones who had lost their way.

School presented a different set of circumstances. It seemed like the least cool profession for a child's parent to have was being a pastor. My classmates' parents were doctors, firemen, lawyers, policemen, corporate executives, flight attendants, and restaurant owners. When I couldn't avoid the question any longer, I would say, "My parents are in ministry."

At that time, there was no clear frame of reference to explain full-time ministry. This was before the days of Joel Osteen, Joyce Meyer, and Rick Warren. This was long before my father's name became well-known to most people. The Internet wasn't a huge phenomenon accessible to most kids yet. They couldn't just Google my father's name and learn the full scope of our ministry. Most kids didn't even realize that there was a need for the doors of a church to be open on any day other than Sunday. So in school we were just Cora and Sarah.

Some of the parents and teachers knew, of course, but hardly any of the kids seemed to know or care. Most of them did not attend our church, nor did they spend their time watching television broadcasts of other churches. There was no way they could understand what it was like for people to stop us in the halls at church on Sunday and tell us our dad said something that literally saved their lives.

I'm not sure I fully understood or appreciated our parents' ministry myself. I just knew that I often got tired of going to the church to do the same thing over and over again. Sure, it was nice spending time with our friends and making jokes throughout the services, but the heart of our family's mission was often lost on me. I just felt like we went to church for a living. And despite the fact that my parents loved helping people, it was hard work.

Few understood the work that goes into ministry, the preparation necessary to prepare a safe place for people to come and have a corporate encounter with God. And even though our church was larger than ever before, at the time it only meant there was more to do. When the doors of The Potter's House opened, my parents had to make sure the lights were on, the bathrooms were stocked, and the vans were gassed for the homeless ministry.

Someone had to run background checks on the volunteers in children's church. The sanctuary must be cleaned and cleared of the remaining tissues from the funeral last week. The carpet must be vacuumed from the wedding on Saturday. The women's ministry must raise funds to host an event for the ladies in the church.

Then there are all the ministries outside the church. Ministering in our communities throughout the greater Dallas–Fort Worth area is a full-time job in itself. Preparing for international mission trips to extend help and share faith around the world required more than just a Sunday meeting after church. While they had lots of help, my parents were ultimately responsible.

They knew and taught us through their example that to whom much is given, much is required. The larger their stage grew, the more they were intent on serving. And our stage was definitely growing. Hundreds of new people, and eventually thousands, began joining our church.

The ministry's growth didn't keep us from finding a way to wreak a little havoc. Cora and I, along with our baby brother and older twin brothers, spent most of our summers roaming around the church while our parents worked. Too young to be trusted with anything important around the church, we found our own way to further our entrepreneurial endeavors. My good ol' partner in crime, Cora, and I were soon back to our usual scheming.

Early one weekday morning, before all the staff of aunts and uncles came in, we were at the church with our mom. As she prepared for her day, we grabbed our backpacks and went to the kitchen. Usually we would watch television, color, or play games for a while, but not this time. With our backpacks in tow, Cora and I emptied out our piggy banks and bought all the snacks out of all the vending machines.

Our plan was simple. We were going to raise the price and sell them back to the staff. Other kids had lemonade stands; we had vending machines. Of course, our profitability was short-lived, even if our ingenuity was well respected.

In the quiet hallways of our church, surrounded by the fifty families from West Virginia that relocated with us, we were reminded of home. Unlike Sundays, when thousands of families swarmed us, these familiar faces knew us too well to be mystified by our presence. They understood that we were just kids, my parents just people.

Like most children at that age, I understood the basic fundamentals of our faith, but its necessity wasn't always apparent. I wouldn't learn until much later that the value of constantly going to church as a child is to remind you where to go in times of trouble as an adult. But when you are young and go to church more days in a week than you attend school, church becomes a competition. Who dressed the best? Who could shout the loudest? Who could sing the best? Who was the best at imitating this elder or that deacon? These were the games that we played all service long.

One of my first true encounters with God came on a Sunday evening service when we hosted a guest pastor. Toward the end of the message, the congregation was visibly moved. After engaging in intense worship, the visiting pastor looked at one of our family friends and spoke directly to a situation in her life. There was no way he could have known those things, as their paths had never crossed.

The moment he pointed his hand toward her, everyone around us stretched out their arms to them, signifying corporate prayer. Something about that moment made me stretch out my small hands, too. I wasn't sure exactly what the sermon text had been or even the title of the sermon. I did understand, however, that the atmosphere had completely shifted. Something was different.

It was as if, for the first time, I understood what it was like to be connected to Someone greater than myself. I felt the presence of God before I knew it was Him. Of course, we would laugh and maybe joke about it later, but I knew that what I felt was real. I just didn't know the day would come when it wouldn't be so easy to find Him in my life.

Even those times when we didn't understand our parents' praise, we could feel their worship. Those were the moments when the soil of our souls was tilled, and God honored the prayers of our family by placing a seed inside of us. It would be many years and many battles before any of us would see whether our giggles turned into silence, silence into whispers, and whispers into prayers.

When you grow up in church, you never know whether those seeds will actually develop into anything. Will they fall on rocky ground? Or will they take root and send a tender shoot peeking through the ground? Over the course of the years, I've seen so many of our friends lose their way and never come back to church. We publicly play into the speculation, wondering where things went wrong for them, but secretly we know it could just as easily be us.

The soil of our souls was tilled, and God honored the prayers of our family by placing a seed inside of us.

In youth service we sat in a circle, said a phrase, and passed it on. By the time the phrase reached the last person, the original message was almost always distorted. It was how we learned the danger of rumors. At the same time, this game was being played in the adult service. Except there, the messages weren't always distorted. During group trips with friends to the bathroom, I'd overhear that the lady on the front pew just got out of jail. Or while helping set up for the next service, I'd learn that one of the deacons had just left his wife. Sometimes they were shameful truths, like mine would soon become; they were the secrets we tell and the crosses we bear when the hymns are over and the benediction has come to an end.

Because of those moments of whispered half-truths, I always had one desire:

Avoid the tales of the pews.

At a young age I learned that people smile big, hug tight, and then go home and drown in their tears. I learned that sometimes you go to church to be healed, but if you aren't careful, the people's approval can become more important than the message. As much as I didn't want to be a whisper, a rumor, or a stare, I soon discovered this would be very difficult for me to avoid. I didn't want to risk exposing an inevitable flaw and being observed under such intense scrutiny.

But it wouldn't be long before my name would be the one passed around.

When we were all children, singing in the choir was par for the course, but when we got into our teenage years, they held auditions for solos and even the choir itself. Turns out I'm not much of a singer. Once while singing in the youth choir, I couldn't remember the words for the life of me. It was okay, though; since I knew it had to be about Jesus, I just hummed along and made up my own words. This plan worked beautifully until the song ended abruptly. There I was still singing words that had nothing to do with that song's lyrics in a pitch that would make the quietest of dogs bark.

To this day, I haven't reconciled that I honestly and truly cannot sing. I don't mean that I just shouldn't have a solo, either. I mean that I shouldn't be allowed within a hundred feet of a microphone. Yes, it's that bad.

How tragic that we

often allow the image

of perfection to cloud

the need to show where

His strength was made

perfect in us.

As if my lack of vocal talent wasn't enough, it turns out my rhythm wasn't that great, either. That ruled out anything music-related; and honestly, reading the Bible didn't seem all that interesting at that age, so I couldn't imagine myself preaching like my father.

I was content to fade into the background of the spotlight.

There in the shadows backstage, I stuck with the people I knew, the ones who were like me, still finding how they could fit into the roles that we saw played before us each Sunday. We looked at ourselves. Our thoughts, emotions, and feelings accelerated us toward young adulthood. It became difficult to understand how we could play church *and* conquer temptation. So instead of fighting the flesh and rising to the standard of what it appeared Christianity required, we chose to be ourselves. We began the mission to explore fully the limits of our humanity before sacrificing them for the politics of church whispers.

Having only been exposed to our limited worldview of church and adolescence, we had no way of knowing that the whispers would come anyway, even outside the church. Isn't it amazing how we can hear the booming voice of the preacher, the sound of instruments blaring, and our choirs singing with gusto and still all we hear are the whispers?

We focus so closely on the whispers that we miss the overall message. As Christians we must strive to be like Christ, never forgetting that the word *strive* suggests struggle. We are all imperfect and no one is without flaws, and fortunately, ministry isn't about leading people to ourselves. It's about leading them back to the One who saved us. How tragic that we often allow the image of perfection to cloud the need to show where His strength was made perfect in us.

Entering adolescence, I was the least likely of the five Jakes children to ever be in ministry. I saw the toll it took on my parents to subject their lives to the needs of other people. I heard the things they said—usually what other people were saying about them—when they thought we weren't listening. And as their ministry reached more and more people, and their stature in the public spotlight grew, we read the stories in the news. I couldn't imagine how the long days, lengthier nights, and relentless scrutiny of people were worth it.

In 2001, my father was named America's Best Preacher by *Time* magazine. I was thirteen years old, and suddenly there was only one question everyone wanted to ask me: "Are you going to be a preacher like your dad?" I hardly knew what I was going to wear to school the next day, much less whether or not I ever wanted to become America's Best Preacher.

With no visible route into ministry, I dedicated myself to my studies and hanging with my friends. Though some of them possessed the talents displayed throughout the church, many of them weren't comfortable fitting in traditional molds. Sometimes it's easier to never go down a path than to risk being rejected. But just because it's easy doesn't mean it's right.

I have seen countless people hurt by church because they didn't fit the acceptable roles. Whether it was the things they whispered to themselves or what they heard whispered about others, some people stifled their voices, talents, and ideas because they knew their ideas were too innovative. When our youth ministry wanted to take popular songs we heard on the radio and give them a Christian twist, the older members of our congregation looked like they had been personally attacked. It seemed like the idea of updating our traditions so that we could attract a younger audience was out of the question. No wonder we doubted ourselves and our contributions.

Our insecurities create holes inside us that make us believe we can't be used. In our everyday lives, change is celebrated. Manufacturers remodel their vehicles to create sleeker and edgier designs.

> *So often people cling to ideas of perfection and lose the innovation that someone who recognizes their areas of growth can bring.*

Cell phones once considered a luxury have become a necessity and home landlines seem like quaint antiques. The world is constantly evolving around us. Creativity brims in every area of our lives, but it isn't always accepted within the traditions of our church walls. So often people cling to ideas of perfection and lose the innovation that someone who recognizes their areas of growth can bring.

How, then, can we teach a generation that transformation doesn't come overnight and that the process may be difficult, but with God we never struggle in vain? This message has been lost on so many people who have the heart to serve but then also carry the shame of mistakes that makes them hide.

I know because I was one of them.

In 1973, *An American Family* debuted on PBS. The television show was revolutionary for its time. It centered around the Louds, a seemingly normal family that had sensational secrets. Over time, the show covered a range of situations the family encountered, from the parents announcing their decision to divorce to their son revealing that he was gay. This show is often considered the first foray into reality television.

It was undoubtedly the beginning of a phenomenon. Millions of people were enthralled with the idea that people who looked relatively normal on the outside struggled with these incredible secrets behind closed doors. Now more than forty years later, reality television has documented almost every aspect of a person's life. From *Survivor* to *Swamp People*, *Big Brother* to *The Bachelor*, and *Sister Wives* to yes, *Preachers' Daughters*, we have found a certain comfort in realizing that, in spite of all the nuances that divide us, trouble does not escape any of us.

If our favorite celebrity or our next-door neighbor has their own set of problems and crises, then it helps us see that we are not alone. Unfortunately, we don't always share this message when we talk about our walk with Christ.

> *In spite of all the nuances that divide us, trouble does not escape any of us.*

As an adolescent, I didn't see anyone serving in ministry who vocalized how I felt. I wanted to understand how you get from point A to point B. I wanted to believe that there were other people like me in the pews of the church. People who ached with intense emotions and didn't always understand why they did what they did. People who made mistakes even while longing to do the right thing.

It was easy to find someone to create mischief with. It proved to be a bit more difficult to find someone willing to admit that they wanted to do right, to be a better person, but had no idea how to start.

When you're a teenager, how do you determine what being a Christian looks like if someone doesn't offer to be as transparent as the reality television world we live in? If we are to make it easier for others to find God, we must be more diligent about sharing our stories—openly and honestly. As I looked around our weekly church gatherings, I couldn't find the trail of bread crumbs between the two worlds, church and reality.

If we discuss only our victories and not our struggles, we allow others to believe that you can win a war without engaging in battle. In fact, it is winning the small fights that allows us the grace to win the ultimate battle: finding a way to use our insecurities and pain to fuel God's purpose for our life.

> *If we discuss only our victories and not our struggles, we allow others to believe that you can win a war without engaging in battle.*

Like others who were unclear on where they fit in the world or how they could squeeze into the preconceived notions of what a Christian should be, I had to find my own way.

Outside of being T.D. Jakes's daughter, I still had yet to discover who Sarah was. Fortunately, when it came down to guiding me, my parents were my parents first and my spiritual leaders second. I know this must seem completely reasonable from the outside looking in, but so many pastors' kids get lost in the shadow of the church. Somehow, though, I think my parents understood that forcing God on us would not be nearly as effective as our finding Him on our own.

For many who grow up in the church, the moment they recite a Scripture, sing a hymn, pick up drumsticks, or hit a note on the piano, they are thrust into ministry. Yet so many of these same children end up resenting ministry as adults. When they encounter the kind of trouble that often leads others closer to God, they can't admit their struggles because of their position in the church. Instead, they feel they have no choice but to forsake their position and the church.

How can we learn about grace every Sunday, but when the teacher needs it, we send them away? Surely if doctors can catch colds and lawyers can be sued, ministers must find themselves needing grace. To say that pastors' kids can't get in trouble is like telling a policeman he should never have to call 9-1-1. Just because you help others doesn't mean you never need help yourself.

Just because you help others doesn't mean you never need help yourself.

And I was about to need a *lot* of help. So much that it would take my family's faith to the breaking point. Not yet fourteen, I discovered I was pregnant.

2

New Worlds

WHEN I WAS thirteen, I felt trapped in between worlds. Not just the worlds of church life and real life, but the worlds of being a little girl and being a grown woman. Of being a Jakes and being just Sarah. Sometimes I still liked watching kids' shows or even cartoons. Other times I was fascinated by adult dramas featuring complicated love triangles. Sometimes it was still fun to play video games with Cora and my brothers. Other times, I wanted to shop for perfume at the mall. And, of course, like every teenage girl, I worried about what to wear. I didn't want to look like a kid, but there was no way my parents would let me dress as chic as the models in *Essence*, *Allure*, and *Seventeen*.

Our family's sheltered lifestyle probably made me more curious about life outside of the pews and our home. I was intrigued by how life seemed to mold people into thinking and living a certain way. So I read novels about peer pressure and the journey of finding yourself and often envied the liberty their characters enjoyed. The girls in these stories weren't held to the standard of perfect Christ-like behavior. It seemed like they were allowed to just be normal. To make mistakes and have arguments with their parents and date the school bad boy and to then learn and grow and just enjoy their lives. I wanted so badly to be this kind of normal, free of judgment and the constant evaluation of others.

One of my favorites was the Sweet Valley High series of books, which chronicled the lives of twin sisters Elizabeth and Jessica. I was immediately drawn to their characters because, most of my life, Cora and I were confused for twins. When you grow up close in age with someone, people often expect you both to grow into the same type of person. While my sister and I were close, we both yearned to be recognized as distinct individuals, like most young adolescents as they leave childhood behind.

The Sweet Valley High books represented the life I thought everyone was living except us. For me, it was a glimpse into the "normal" lives we could have had if our parents had "regular" jobs. Maybe we would still be liked and even popular—not because we were part of the America's Best Preacher's family but because of our radiant personalities and impeccable fashion sense. Or maybe we could fade into the background without anyone ever realizing we disappeared, just doing whatever we wanted without everyone scrutinizing our every move.

I was too young to realize that when you try to live someone else's life, you just trade one problem for another. At the time, the American dream only looked one way—perfect but never boring, innocent but also glamorous, sophisticated but uncomplicated. Almost everything I remember viewing on television or reading in a book centered around this concept that white picket fences should just appear and envelop your life with predictable but never boring happiness.

Once you reached a certain age, pursued higher education, and landed an above-average job, everything else was supposed to just fall in place. In this serene existence, there is no need to look for love or affirmation, because you had your childhood sweetheart, a boy you had watched grow into manhood even as his love for you only grew deeper.

It seemed so attainable for everyone else. As my parents' ministry transformed them into national leaders and international celebrities, I wondered how this preacher's daughter could ever fade so quietly into the background that I could become just a normal girl living a normal life. Like the ones in my books or in the movies, the ones who had it all together, with no one outside of their loving family to answer to, all inside the security of that white picket fence.

"Does he eat dinner with you?" "Does your mom cook?" "How does he talk at home?" "Does he pray all the time?" "Does she really speak so softly?" "Does he have the entire Bible memorized?" "Does he really know Oprah?"

The questions were endless. And they rarely had anything to do with me.

I know it may not seem like a big deal on the outside looking in, but imagine your own journey of trying to find yourself as a young adult. By far, more people began asking me, "What's it like being T.D. Jakes's daughter?" than asking me, "How are you doing?" No matter where we went, the script was the same. In grocery stores, chats never centered around our favorite subject in school, the latest ball game, or who our friends were. Instead people wanted to know if my father would be preaching on Sunday and, if so, about what. If not, who was the visiting pastor and would he be as good as Dad.

A large part of me continued to hope that people wanted to get to know me because of something funny I said or an intriguing insight

I had. I wanted to share my love of writing and my favorite dishes to cook, to talk about the ending of that movie I just saw or about the exotic places I longed to visit. Having someone interested in your life is one thing, but I grew tired of having entire conversations about what my parents were like at home.

Right around the age most teenagers believe the world should revolve around them—which I was working hard to make happen—the *Time* cover story on my father hit the stands. Our teachers at school smiled and buzzed about the latest celebrity children in their classrooms—me and Cora. Somehow I missed the part in Sweet Valley High where the teachers ask Jessica or Elizabeth to pray for their grandmother. Or when their parent-teacher conferences turn into counseling sessions about the teacher's own childhood issues.

Before you label me an ungrateful brat, please understand. I know that being a pastor or a preacher is a gift. I've always felt like it was the ability to translate God's Word to His people. When you're bogged down with your own life dramas, speaking to someone who hears so clearly from God can make a huge difference. The only problem is that when your father is named America's Best Preacher, the world becomes his congregation—one which seemed not only to surround me but to close in on me a little more each day.

It's unfortunate and quite sad that some people occasionally step on a pastor's family in an attempt to touch the hem of his garment. Many of them mean well (and some don't) as they seek to improve their own self-worth by associating with someone they perceive as God's solution to their problems. I became instantly leery of those people. I didn't want to believe that the only way God could heal them was by hurting us.

On Sundays at church, adults would stop us in the hallway to deliver a message to our father. Often confusing me with my sister, they would yell, "Cora!" and then chastise me for not answering. It was becoming clearer that I hardly fit into the church machine, yet because of my family's ties to the church, and my father's newfound fame, I couldn't truly fit in with my school friends.

So there I stood. Not just in between two worlds but on the verge of a whole new solar system.

————

We once had a man visit our church who spent decades in prison for a crime he did not commit. As he gave his testimony in church one Sunday, he talked about how difficult it was for him to adjust to freedom again. When he was first imprisoned, cell phones did not exist. Technology hadn't advanced to the heights it had reached by the time he spoke at our church. He entered prison as part of one world and left it to return to another world he barely recognized.

The incredible thing about his story is that he never gave up. He knew he was innocent. He knew he didn't belong there, but he did the best he could to keep going. Every day he had a choice, he said, to be grateful for life or to despair and die. He chose to live and to make the most of his life even behind concrete walls and iron bars. I listened as he talked about the friendships he formed,

So there I stood. Not just in between two worlds but on the verge of a whole new solar system.

the positive mentality he adapted, and the irony that he was among those incarcerated but more liberated than any of them. He said that inmates were not the only ones imprisoned in our world.

In many ways I understood. Growing up in church can sometimes feel like a prison. I'm not trying to sound irreverent or disrespectful. It's simply that many people in church expect you to conduct yourselves according to their rules. If you break them in anyway, you are subject to a punishment of their choice. For some, it's having to apologize in front of the entire congregation. Others are told to be seen and not heard for the remainder of their life. Usually, their rules and punishments are accompanied by a claiming of the authority of God.

Despite my parents' best attempts to make our church a place of healing, freedom, and joy, there were still some people among the thousands of members committed to their own agendas. And of course, the church leader and his family were held to the highest standards and levels of scrutiny by these people.

On the outside it may not seem that bad. Once a week you're alienated for a couple of hours, but it is so much more than that. The people who punish you are usually the ones you thought would help you to get back on your feet. It's a tricky thing to watch strangers come to the altar and receive a hug and prayer, but when it's your turn they tell you to hide your pain.

So when it was me who needed the prayer, I didn't say a word.

For what felt like a long time, I searched for myself in the eyes of other people, hoping someone would ask me the questions I so desperately wanted to be able to answer: "Who are you?" "Who are you apart from being the daughter of Bishop Jakes and the First Lady of The Potter's House?" "What are you really like inside?" "What do you want to do with your life?"

I had found a temporary home straddling the fence of the familiar roles of church, even while peeking at the allure of the mysterious world that seemed to beckon. But finally I began to take those first few steps of exploration. This new place offered freedom. No expectations of perfection. No whispered judgments and knowing eyes. If I wanted to discover who Sarah was, then I knew it would be outside the walls of our church.

So in an effort to find myself, I did what most teenagers do: tried my hardest to become everything I saw as grown-up, mature, adult, and independent. If I was no longer a little girl, then I must be an adult. Which meant rehearsing the experiences that make you a grown-up, at least according to my friends. Little did I know that peer pressure very rarely has an age limit. So many of us spend our whole lives trying to become who we think everyone else is. We hardly ever realize everyone else is just pretending, too.

I didn't get to maintain my secret rebellion against church members' expectations for long. Time would quickly tell my truth. Soon everyone would know I was pregnant just weeks before my fourteenth birthday. With each tiny flutter in my stomach, I knew that soon I would be falling on my knees at the mercy of the church court.

So many of us spend our whole lives trying to become who we think everyone else is. We hardly ever realize everyone else is just pretending, too.

Today, I don't remember a time when I didn't have my son. From the moment I held him in my arms, it was like everything that happened before him was lost in the hopes of his future. Before I reach the age of thirty, I will have spent more of my life as a mother than not. And while I wish that I could've honored the beauty that is his soul with a more traditional entrance into the world, the truth is . . . he saved me.

My son forced me to find myself. Because of him I learned that there are worse things than not fitting in. Living a lie is much worse.

These realizations didn't come easy, though.

When I was a kid, I used to wonder why adults always hugged children when they got hurt. It seemed so silly. Why would you use your arms to wrap them around someone's torso when they hurt their toe? It seemed like it would make much more sense to pay attention to the specific area that absorbed the trauma.

When I was thirteen, I learned why. A child finds pain to be momentary. Within minutes, children's cries can turn from a bloodcurdling scream to heart-swelling laughter. For children, the hug shows them that we're sorry they got hurt, but we know they'll be okay. As you grow older, the hugs take on quite a few more meanings.

When you're dealing with death, we hug as a way to show our sympathy. It shows that we recognize that we are incapable of touching the hurt. Still, with arms wrapped around a broken heart, we hope that just for a moment we can hold someone together at a time they feel like they are falling apart the most. Unlike when we were children, we can no longer leave someone with the reassurance that things will go back to normal within minutes. Instead, all we have to offer is a drop of love in a drought of despair.

One of my greatest fears when I first learned I was pregnant was that I would be in trouble with my parents. I assumed that my pregnancy would be like bringing home Fs in all of my classes. Up to that point I had never done anything that would alter the trajectory of my life. Sure, Cora and I got into mischief from time to time, but that was a long time ago, kid's stuff. Flunking classes on your report card can hardly compare to an unplanned teen pregnancy, but at that time in my life I did not have much to compare it to. Despite my best efforts, I was still that girl trying to find her place among the many worlds circling around her.

As much as I longed to be an independent woman, free of the opinions of others, I was still a child myself, struggling to navigate bridges between worlds. I wanted to be the girl everyone loved. With very few recognizable talents at that age, I depended on the popularity of who I was. As you may remember, I couldn't sing. I wasn't the best dancer. I liked to talk, to get to know someone, even if they only seemed interested in asking the same questions about my family. All I had was the superficial clout of being the Bishop's daughter, the child of a man making history. It was all that I knew about myself. It was all that others seemed to care about. So I took on the role, but not the responsibility.

I had a small group of friends who, like me, were too cool to be in church, too naïve to be in the world. We laughed at our peers who were so on fire for God because we didn't understand the exact moment when we were no longer playing church. Little by little, though, our large group dwindled down. The laughs and giggles once shared on the back pews murmured down until it was just about six of us.

Each of us paired up with a childhood love—the one we hoped would turn into the co-owner of our white-picket-fence fantasy. Mine, only a year older than me, had been coming to the church with his family for years. An attraction was there, more of infatuation by default than a burning romantic love.

My friends and I had perfected the art of sitting in an area of the sanctuary that would allow us to look like we were actively listening during the service while we were actually just catching up or making future plans. We all had to be there, but we all began to discover this strange new world of our teen years together.

For a while it seemed to work. I had found a way to fit in and still go unnoticed. I went to church but didn't participate. I sat with a small group of peers consistently. Being their pastor's daughter naturally made me the leader of the pack. At the time I had no clue that a leader without direction is dangerous. Instead of using the influence to challenge us to become better, more diligent, and immersed

A leader without direction is dangerous.

in God's Word, I became more like the world around us. The blind leading the blind.

I knew the expectations were for me to set the standard. Whether it was clothing, jewelry, music, or movies, I decided that I would have to gain my friends' respect by constantly staying on the cutting edge. I was the one leading our expedition into adolescence. So when we became teenagers and started having puppy love relationships and schoolyard crushes, it seemed like sex was the natural next step.

Three months later, I learned the cost of my exploration.

I knew long before I took a test on Easter of 2002 that I was pregnant. The signs came long before the plus sign appeared. Mainly, my cycles stopped coming nearly three months before I took the test. I was unusually tired, and the smell of some of my favorite foods began to nauseate me.

Still, I hoped that I had made a miscalculation or that the early-pregnancy symptoms were actually being caused by stress and not the life growing inside of me. I didn't know the first thing about raising a baby or being a parent. It simply didn't seem possible.

I stared at the pregnancy test, knowing that my life would be changed forever. I just had no way of knowing how.

Our Sunday ritual of sitting in the back, catching up on each other's weeks, became my time for silent strategy meetings. *What will I do? Who should I tell? When should I tell? What in the world is going to happen after I tell?*

My sister was the first person I confided in. Cora would also be the first person wise enough—or brave enough—to tell my parents. The day that she told them, I hardly remember any words that were said. Torn between her loyalty to me and her responsibility as a big sister, Cora wrote a letter about my pregnancy and left it in the mailbox. But since we didn't actually receive mail at the house, our parents knew it was from one of us. I couldn't deny the letter and I couldn't blame my sister. Based on my calculations, I was nearly four months along. The situation wasn't going to go away, no matter how much I ignored it.

That night all six of us—my parents, Cora, Jermaine, Jamar, and I—sat in our living room for hours as a family. They needed answers. I had questions. We needed grace. I poured out all of my insecurities and answered as many questions as I could. I took in their shock. We made no plans for what was next. There was no time for that. I think we rested from the pressure of having to hold it all together. Instead, we took a moment to break down.

I went to my room that night, and it seemed with each step up the stairs my stomach grew more and more. It all became a reality. I crawled into my bed, drained from the emotions of the day. With my head on my pillow, I closed my eyes and cried. Their faces, shocked with grief and amazement, haunted me each time I closed my eyes. I replayed the conversation we'd just had over and over in my head, their soft, stunned voices asking me the next question. I could only try to drown the memories with my tears.

I felt a hand on my back rubbing in a soft, familiar circular motion. Then I heard Jermaine whispering everything would be okay. I fell asleep crying in his lap and woke up to his hand still glued to my back.

Over the course of the following week, I remember my family hugging me and hugging each other often. For the first time I realized the difference between a momentary struggle and a lifetime journey. My changing body being held together by their arms made me realize that this was so much bigger than being grounded.

You see, I got pregnant before our televisions were inundated with reality shows. I had no concept of what being a teen mom meant. I honestly don't think I understood that my actions would affect not just me but the child inside of me, too. I didn't know that I had crossed the bridge from childhood hugs to an adult embrace. No longer were they hugging me because in minutes I would be fine. Instead, they were hugging me because the road ahead of me was uncertain. They were hugging me because it was all they could do.

Some people learn worship by watching others. Others learn it by experiencing a struggle so great they have no other way to release the relentless shame, the terrifying fear, or unbearable pain.

I still didn't understand the ministry fully. I hadn't yet faced an obstacle that required the type of worship that I was surrounded by each Sunday. I could feel God's presence, but I had no wounds to offer up for Him to heal.

Some people learn worship by watching others. Others learn it by experiencing a struggle so great they have no other way to release the relentless shame, the terrifying fear, or unbearable pain. As someone in the latter category, I had my first adult encounter with God when I was a child, carrying a child, and pleading for grace.

The days following the revelation of my pregnancy were all filled with silence. It was how I knew that I was facing something that even my parents weren't sure how to process.

When you miss an assignment or stay up past your bedtime, the parental words seem endless, because the consequences are evident. When you learn your child is having a child, though, I have to imagine it leaves you a bit speechless.

After the initial shock wore off, the first thing my mother did was take me to the doctor. I did not know how far along I was or what restrictions my pregnancy would involve.

The car ride to the doctor was the loudest silence I had ever heard. Swarming between us in the seats of my mother's car were all the words that were left unsaid. I was scared in a way I had never experienced before.

I had never been in the kind of trouble that begat silence. My father is a preacher, my mother a drama enthusiast. They love language and are articulate people. There were few times when our home was rendered to silence. Like when my grandmother became ill and started living with us or the day we came home from school and learned our granny had passed away. Until my pregnancy, death had been the only agent powerful enough to render the walls of our home silent.

In many ways, I believe we were grieving the loss of a dream. Not many kids dream of becoming parents before they're even able to drive. Most parents don't imagine they'll be grandparents while their children are still in high school. But this was our reality.

In an effort to protect our privacy, the doctor allowed us to come in around closing time. The doctor informed us that one of the first things we would have to determine was how far along I was. After taking my blood, checking my blood pressure, and running test after test, the doctor took me to another room.

Once I heard the hum of the monitor and saw the familiar utensils on the table, I knew that I was going to see my baby for the first time. Slowly, I walked to the table. A part of me was excited to actually

Until my pregnancy,

death had been the only

agent powerful enough

to render the walls

of our home silent.

see the life inside of me. The other part of me wished I could offer him more than a confused teenager trying to find her way.

The cool gel spread across my stomach and chills went up my spine. It didn't seem possible that this could be real, but I knew my limited mind could have never imagined this moment.

And then . . . there it was.

With the lights dimmed and our faces turned to the monitor, I saw my baby for the first time. Floating in the safety of my womb, this precious soul had no idea that I was thirteen. The baby didn't know that I was T.D. Jakes's daughter. Inside of me there was no danger of my baby being a casualty of church politics. No, this life could not fathom what kind of world was waiting.

Even when we don't always feel safe, what's inside of us is protected. Our destiny, our future, the key to who we are is protected even when we feel the least safe.

As my mother held my hand, I felt a single teardrop fall in the crack between our hands. That tear mixed with the sweat of our nerves, the excitement of a new life, the fear of an uncertain future, and a promise that no matter what I wasn't alone. The doctor asked if we wanted to know the gender of the baby, and instantly I said yes.

I was having a boy.

The girliest girl on the planet, I would be bringing a son into the world. I had no name picked out in the back of my mind and no intuitive, maternal sense of what to do. I wasn't even sure that I *could* do this. It's one thing to have a baby. It's another to have a baby at fourteen—and beyond comprehensible to become a parent with thousands of people watching you.

After Cora knew but before she told our parents, I told my small group of friends. They tried to imagine how drastically my life would change. One of the older girls who hung out with us was the first to mention that my life didn't have to change.

"You don't have to keep the baby, you know," she said.

I looked at her quizzically. "Really?" I asked.

"Sure, it may leave you a little hurt on the inside, but you can have a normal life if you get an abortion or give it up for adoption." She looked at me knowingly. "Almost like it never happened."

The thought of giving birth to my son and then later looking into the eyes of a little boy on the street and wondering if he was mine would kill me. I didn't feel strong enough to do that. And the moment I heard his rapid heart beating inside of me and saw him darting from side to side inside my womb, I knew that I couldn't end his life just so that I could live "normally"—if such a thing were even possible.

So here I was, almost fourteen and pregnant.

For almost a year before my pregnancy, my siblings and I were being homeschooled. With my parents' busy travel schedules and the increasingly difficult politics of growing up Jakes, it seemed like being at home was the best choice.

Which helped now, because I didn't have to explain my growing stomach to my teachers and classmates. It was as if God was protecting me from the added trouble my insecurities would bring. I was pregnant for nine months with my son, but it would take much longer for me to birth the woman I was becoming. As I look back, I'm convinced my pregnancy was the only way God could truly slow me down enough to show me who I really am. In many ways I was developing a son and God was developing Sarah.

In an effort to prepare for becoming a mother, I became completely secluded. Surrounded mostly by my family and close friends, I focused on my schooling, health, and learning all that I could about parenting.

After the initial shock of my pregnancy wore off, my parents became my coaches. My father told me, "You can recover from this, but you're going to have to hit the ground running." I knew that he was worried about me.

My own birth had been a shock to my parents. My sister was not quite three months old when my mother learned she was pregnant with me. For years after I was born, I was completely engrossed in my role as the baby of our family. My mother loves to retell the stories of me asking my father for something and him stopping whatever he was doing to get it for me.

When I was a little girl, maybe five or six years old, we were driving home from a late-night service at our church in West Virginia. Tired after such a long day, my sister and I cuddled up in the back seat of my parents' Lincoln. We were both fast asleep in minutes, but I started waking up because I was cold.

In the front, my mother and father were having an adult discussion. You know, one of the ones you know you shouldn't interrupt unless it's an emergency. They were recapping the day's service and catching up with one another, but soon I began to shiver. Lifting myself up a little, making my head visible in the rearview mirror, I whispered, "Daddy, I'm cold."

I tried to whisper softy enough that I wouldn't get in trouble for interrupting. Instantly, my dad stopped talking, looked back at me, and began urgently removing his jacket while driving. It was as if I had told him I was freezing inside an igloo instead of experiencing a slight chill. "Here you go, baby," he said.

But now no jacket could protect me from the cold front of my life circumstances. Despite my parents' best efforts, they could not cover me from the hateful stares, questions, rumors, gossip, and challenges I would face raising a child while not being much more than a child myself. They vowed to face it all with me, though. Their loving support never wavered.

Together huddled in the safety of our home, my parents, brothers, and sister created a womb that would protect me while I developed into a mother. It was clear they loved me fiercely and unconditionally. It was one of the unexpected blessings during that season of uncertainty.

> *No jacket could protect me from the cold front of my life circumstances.*

I turned fourteen on July 17 and was due to give birth on October 18, 2002. Usually, Cora and I celebrated our birthdays with dozens of girls sleeping over, at the movies, bowling, or in some other grand fashion. That year, I sat at the round table in my parents' bedroom surrounded by my siblings and one small blue box.

Strangely enough, even without the typical party, that celebration meant more to me than almost any birthday up to then. At a time when my family had every reason to not celebrate my life, they still took the opportunity to let me know how much I mattered. It reminded me that there were some things my pregnancy had not changed.

During those months before my son was born, I learned more about my family than any Sunday at church had ever showed me. I learned that life may require us to take different paths, but we'll always find our way home, back to each other.

They helped me prepare for my son's arrival. My mother helped convert a portion of my room into a nursery. My sister helped me keep track of my progress by reading all kinds of pregnancy books. My brothers helped me put things like cribs and strollers together and transport me to doctor's appointments. My mother never missed an opportunity to pray over me. My father simply loved me and protected me from the aftermath that the pregnancy might have on the ministry.

As grateful as I was for the support of my family, I knew I had potentially hurt us severely. I knew that everyone's life would somehow be affected by my actions. I wanted to believe they were there because they loved me and not because they felt chained to me.

How could they forgive me when I couldn't forgive myself?

3

Motherhood

IT DIDN'T TAKE long for my pregnancy to be classified as high risk. I was placed on bed rest months before delivery because my body could not handle the stress of my growing son. Of course, I didn't need a doctor to tell me my pregnancy was high risk—everything about it seemed to be stretching me beyond my limits.

Before I was restricted to being home, I still attended service on Sunday. I sat in the main sanctuary with the adults. I wanted to rebuild my parents' trust and prepare myself for the rapid pace at which I would now be forced to grow up. I figured that sitting in the main sanctuary would help me learn more about the experiences of broken people.

After all, I felt like I was broken, damaged goods.

Before, in our youth services, church had been fun. As kids, we really hadn't been through enough of life's hardships to really understand worship. I'm convinced our worship is most beautiful when we are desperate for an answer from God, when we have nothing else to lose, nowhere else to go. When we are completely and utterly lost, that's when our worship is most powerful.

In my own way, while I sat in the main sanctuary, I pleaded with God to find me.

I never felt like I truly needed Him before that time. I figured that when I was ready to grow up and my fun was over, then I would become more serious about my relationship with God. But what I didn't realize is that I was never really hiding from Him. God was there with me the entire time.

One of the first stories most Christians learn about is the fall of man. In the garden of Eden, when Adam and Eve ate the forbidden fruit, one of their first reactions to their newfound reality was to cover their naked bodies. They once lived in the garden with nothing to be ashamed of, certainly not their unclothed bodies. However, the moment they knew they had broken the rules, they immediately covered themselves.

> *Our worship is most beautiful when we are desperate for an answer from God.*

Isn't it funny how quickly shame sets in? Sure, Eve knew what she was doing was wrong, but there's such a huge difference between thinking of doing something and the actual action and its consequences. It's not that you think you're invincible; it's just that you think you won't get sunk in. We believe that we can try something without allowing it to own us. We hardly ever realize things have gone too far until we're ready to hide behind an entire closet full of fig leaves.

Like Eve, I, too, wanted to hide. But anytime my eyes drifted to my stomach, I knew that hiding this secret would be impossible. What do you do when you can't avoid the challenges of your consequences? It seemed to me I had three options: stop living altogether, merely exist in silence, or somehow dare to live again.

By May, our closest friends and family knew I was pregnant, but no one else. That would change at our Mother's Day service. Per our custom, that Sunday my father acknowledged the sacrifice, dedication, and commitment that mothers have made for their children. As my eyes scanned the crowd of nodding heads, tearful eyes, and proud smiles, I wondered if I could do it. Could I really be the kind of mother we were all thinking of and honoring at that moment? I realized then I didn't just want to have a son; I wanted to be a mother.

Was it even possible for a fourteen-year-old girl to be the kind of mother I saw in the pews of the church? From the outside looking in, people always look so well put together. For the first time, I saw beyond the pretty clothes, animated expressions, and lively dancing. I saw the hearts of people who were searching, like me, for some way—any way—they could let God fix their shattered worlds and broken hearts.

My silent reverie was broken when I felt someone pull at my arm, guiding me to stand and be recognized with the other mothers in the congregation. A family friend, one of only a few who knew that I was pregnant, beckoned me to stand to my feet. I had no idea what was going on in the service. I had been too busy searching for a face in the crowd that was like mine. I was looking for hope.

I was too young to realize that on Sundays we all look like we have it together. It's the other days of the week and the tearful nights when our pain seeps to the outside and tells our secrets. We never realize no one has it all together. In that moment I realized I was holding others to the same standard to which I hated being held.

I assumed that they didn't understand me because their faces didn't mirror the turmoil in my soul. Maturity is recognizing that everyone, regardless of race, class, or gender, has something that binds them to the rest of us. It would be years until I realized that even though they may not have been pregnant at thirteen, the mothers in the service that day didn't have a white picket fence either. Some became mothers through rape, while others had been abused or molested. Some were enduring violence at home and others were sick with worry over their children's health and well-being.

On Sundays we all look like we have it together. It's the other days of the week and the tearful nights when our pain seeps to the outside and tells our secrets.

I didn't know their stories, though. So I felt even more isolated than before I got pregnant. Not only would I be separated by my last name, but now I would add being a teen mother to my distinction. In this gathering of people smiling and singing and wearing their Mother's Day corsages, I felt so lost.

I didn't even realize why I had been pulled to stand up until I heard my father repeat that he wanted all the mothers to stand. Instantly, I wanted to disappear. There I was, in front of thousands of people who must be wondering why my young face was standing with all the mothers.

I wasn't even showing at the time, but it didn't take a rocket scientist to figure out that I was going to become someone's mother soon. Eventually, rumors spread throughout the church that I was pregnant. The rumors turned to gossip when my expanding stomach could no longer be concealed. Even the staff who had watched me grow up had their own spin on my truth.

When the doctor placed me on bed rest a few months later, I was relieved I would no longer have to show my face at church. Carrying a facade is always more difficult than embracing the truth. I grew tired of holding it together for everyone observing me while falling apart on the inside. I didn't want to look into disappointed eyes. My ears did not want to overhear "she's the one who's pregnant" when I walked by. I felt safe at home, protected.

I'm sure my pregnancy wasn't the easiest time for my family, especially my parents, but even in their pain they covered me. I tiptoed around the house, aware my stomach was a painful reminder, but I wasn't scared like I was at church. I knew that my parents and siblings loved me. I wasn't sure how we would recover or what my future held, but I was okay here.

As my due date drew closer and the pregnancy became more difficult, like most expectant women, we kept a hospital bag packed and by the door just in case we needed to leave quickly. It seemed ironic that just as I finally began to accept that I was going to become a mother, my body began to threaten the growing life inside of me. I wondered if losing him would be my punishment. But I couldn't bear the thought of not meeting the little person who was taking over my body. During that time I realized

Most women become a mother long before their water breaks. That connection doesn't discriminate with age.

most women become a mother long before their water breaks. That connection doesn't discriminate with age.

I knew that having a child as a teenager was not ideal, to say the least, but I still had the same excitement that any new mother would possess. Nevertheless, I didn't want my excitement to be perceived as being unremorseful, so I kept my feelings to myself. I tried to keep the swirl of mixed emotions inside me and focus on preparations for my soon-to-be new arrival.

Picking baby names, shopping for clothes, choosing strollers and baby bags . . . preparing was so much like playing with my baby doll as a little girl. Only now it was all real. With all the clothes folded and put away, a name selected, and painful kicks, I was being told to prepare for the worst.

I remember after a particularly stressful doctor's appointment, my parents were having a meeting with their attorney about business. So I sat on the stairs of our home waiting for the meeting to conclude. Once I heard the doors open, I asked them all, my parents as well as their lawyer, if I could speak to them for a moment. Taken off guard by my request, they agreed.

Noticeably pregnant at this time, I received an anxious look from the lawyer, who had watched me grow up. I looked them in the eye and asked if we could sign some kind of paper work that would give my parents custody of my son in the event that I died. It was a sobering moment for them, but one I had been considering for quite some time. I knew my pregnancy was very high risk; I saw the look in the doctor's eyes when my condition did not improve. I had read horror stories of girls my age having babies and bleeding out on the table. I didn't know what would happen to my son if something happened to me, but I wanted to cover him before he was even born.

That's when I knew I wouldn't just be a girl who had a baby; I would be a mother. I would gladly sacrifice my life for his own.

They promised they would help me make whatever arrangements were necessary to ensure his safety and well-being. We would all meet in the next week or so to finalize everything. Once all of those arrangements were completed, I finally felt at peace with my upcoming delivery. The night before my scheduled induction, Dexter, eight years old at the time, came and got in the bed with me. I don't know if he was scared of nightmares or if God was just reminding me that I wasn't facing anything alone. Either way, the next morning when I woke up on the floor—Dexter used to sleep like a circus act—I was ready to start my journey as a single mother.

Single, but not alone.

Two weeks before my due date, my doctor had decided the best chance of preserving both my life and the baby's was to induce my labor. I was admitted into the hospital on a Wednesday evening. The induction process started as soon as I was settled that night. Nearly twenty-four hours later, I gave my final push and Malachi came into the world. I chose this name because it means "messenger of God," even though I still wasn't sure exactly what this message would be.

As expected, labor was very difficult. At one point, the doctor could no longer locate the baby's heartbeat, which caused me to panic and sent my body into convulsions. They began to prepare me for a cesarean when suddenly they located the perfect rhythm of his heart.

It turns out having an actual baby is nothing like caring for a baby doll. Our first night in the hospital, sweat dripped down my forehead as I struggled to nurse my son. I felt like I was running a marathon with no finish line in sight. The nurses graciously assisted me each time. I suspect they pitied this young girl who couldn't even feed her son. I didn't have much of a choice, though. I needed their help, and if that came with pity, then I would have to take that, too.

Eventually I got the hang of nursing him without assistance. I used pillows to help me balance his weight and make my body more comfortable. It also took me some time to change his diaper. I couldn't do it as fast as the nurses, afraid that I would hurt his freshly cut skin, but I managed. I never once remember him crying while I was trying to figure out how to be a mother. It was like he knew that I was doing the best I could. His patience with me made me love him more. It made me more committed to not messing up.

Maybe I couldn't give him the life I wanted to, but what if all I had to give him was my heart? Maybe I could be an actual mother after all.

Not only did I put Malachi on a schedule, but I tried my best to become just as regimented. Recognizing now that the fate of his life lay squarely in my own pursuit of success, I committed to doing everything in my power. Before I had my son, I never considered the idea of graduating from high school early, but now I needed to recover more than ever. While a longtime family friend helped with my new baby, I devoted most of my time to completing my studies.

Committed to seeing me succeed, my parents allowed me to attend a more traditional, smaller school where I could take more courses. When I started the tenth grade in the fall of 2003, I had one mission. I wanted to graduate as soon as I could. I wanted to hit the ground running.

Hardly anyone at my small private school knew that I had a son. This fresh start seems like it would have been the perfect scenario for me to fall into having a dual existence. Things were different for me this time, though. Instead of craving attention and popularity, I wanted to hide in the background.

I didn't want to live a lie, so I simply remained silent about my personal life, including Malachi. Among the students, I assumed I was the only one who had a child and once again felt isolated and out of place. With an uncertain future ahead, all I had was my academic ability, so I focused on my studies and worked harder than I would have previously thought possible.

Being only a year apart in age, Cora and I almost always attended the same schools. So she was right beside me when I started attending school as a mother. Although we didn't have the same classes, having her there was like an extension of the security I experienced at home with our family.

Never one to mince words, my sister is notoriously known for speaking her mind. It's what everyone loves about her! You never have to wonder what she thinks or feels. Her candor has often been the source of humorous moments within our family. So one day when we were in the small cafeteria of our high school, Cora's frank personality revealed my secret. And there was nothing subtle about it.

Another classmate of ours was having a heated discussion about teenage mothers with some other students. "I mean, how could they be so stupid," she said. "It would be so much easier to just give it away instead of being selfish and ruining the kid's life."

"Yeah, you said it," agreed another girl. "They already made one mistake. Why make another?" The rest of their group nodded as if she were preaching the gospel.

I sat in the corner, face down, and focused on finishing my lunch. I didn't want to say anything. All she did was vocalize the thoughts I assumed everyone was thinking anyway. I couldn't blame her. They were the thoughts that haunted me at night. The things that made me want to give whatever was left of my future at least my best shot.

"What kind of girl allows herself to get into this kind of trouble anyway?" continued the second girl. Everyone was listening by this point, including my sister.

"Only hos do that!" exclaimed the first girl and laughed.

I sat there soaking in all the thoughts that I knew the world had about me. Instead of standing up for myself, and others like me, I acted as if I were far removed from her subject. Speaking up would only remove my invisible shield.

"WELL, MY SISTER HAD A BABY AND SHE AIN'T A HO!" Cora yelled.

Suddenly, I saw the white light. *This must be what death feels like.* I was *mortified.* Most teenagers experience this moment at least once, usually when their parents embarrass them in front of their friends. But now I was the parent and everyone knew it. Standing in a room full of people who didn't even know my name, I now was forced to accept that they knew my secret.

As if being the only black students in the class didn't make my sister and me minority enough, the fact that our father was a nationally known preacher was even more of a separation. Now the fact that I did my homework while burping my son would create another divide.

I felt the separation everywhere. At home, I felt like a black sheep. Not because anyone made me feel that way but mostly because no one else had done anything to place us all under such heavy scrutiny. My father's ability to effectively minister was brought into question, my mother's commitment to women marred. The overall closeness of our entire family was being investigated by the outside world because of what I did.

My first Sunday back at church, everyone from my brothers to distant cousins came into the service with me. They knew that I was nervous about showing up with my infant son, confirming and enflaming the rumors that were already constantly growing. Some people knew and had been sending letters to the church demanding

It's hard to accept

pure love

when you feel you

don't deserve it.

I apologize publicly or they'd leave the church. My father made sure they knew where the door was located.

I know what you're thinking. How blessed I am to have a father who was willing to stand by me at the expense of losing his position. You're right, but I couldn't see that at the time. All I could do was feel the shame of his even being placed in that situation. It's hard to accept pure love when you feel you don't deserve it. It's essentially what keeps us from maximizing our relationship with Christ. How can salvation be available to a wretch like me? So instead of feeling the comfort of protection on the Sunday of Malachi's debut, I prepared for the sting of shock.

"I'd like to welcome back to service my daughter Sarah and grandson, Malachi." It was all my father ever said about it publicly until several years later, in 2011. Within days the letters started flying in. Some were lending me their strength, others were forsaking my future, and then there were the really ugly ones. The lady who sent me a blanket to wrap my baby in when he died, since she just knew that God was going to take my son from me because he was born out of sin. There were countless more where that came from. Worse than the letters were the stares. The deacon's wife who had once hugged me each time she saw me now made it a point to turn the other way. Taking Chi to children's church was like putting him on display. They wanted to know who his father was, and my silence only fueled assumptions.

I've always felt like my son's relationship with his father is private. We were both so young when Malachi came into the world. I knew that he was still finding his way. Just because my process was on display didn't mean I had to expose his, too. So I've remained committed to that stance ever since.

In between studying and caring for Chi, I began honing my culinary skills. I always enjoyed cooking, but I figured furthering my knack would make me a better mother, daughter, and sister. Without being asked, I began to routinely cook family dinners. I knew on the outside it looked like I was just trying to help, but I also wanted to earn forgiveness. Perhaps if I did so much good on this end, it would make up for the decisions I had made on the other.

There are some people who make mistakes and then immediately confront what hurt them. They do the work because the only way through something is to actually go through the process. Then there are others, like me, who feel like there is no time on their side and they must make the best of what they have left, even if that means driving on a flat tire.

My parents were raised in the hills of West Virginia. They pride themselves on their ability to weave through mountain passes and effortlessly maneuver in the snow. When we moved to Dallas, there weren't any mountains and snow never stayed for long. Instead, they traded mountains for multiple-lane expressways. Most of the major highways that currently exist in Dallas were under construction when we arrived in Texas. It wasn't uncommon for us to see cars on the side of the road with frustrated drivers calling for assistance after running over stray debris.

When my sister and I were learning to drive, one of our family friends would give us driving tips. Among the many things he taught us, like how to change the oil and replace windshield wiper fluid, was how to handle a flat tire. He taught us the basics of tire changing, but realizing that we might panic in the actual event, he left us with one major tip. He said, "Whenever you get a flat tire, pull over to a safe spot as soon as possible. It will feel like you can continue driving, but just because you can go doesn't mean you should. Continuing to drive on a flat tire can cause repair costs to increase significantly."

If only I truly understood what living while damaged would cost me.

So often we'd rather rush our healing so that we can appear to have recovered. From miles away it is nearly impossible to tell whether a passing vehicle's tire has adequate air. Sometimes, only those close to you can recognize when you aren't moving the best you can . . . and then there are times when you are the only one who knows you're damaged. The rhythmic grind of metal against metal serves as a reminder that you're moving, but you have been punctured.

If only I truly understood what living while damaged would cost me.

Having my son knocked the air out of me. I was driving through life on a flat tire. I thought that reaching my goal was more important than checking on my own damage. I didn't have time to stop because I was already behind. I wish I had known that no matter how much we numb our pain, it never truly goes away. Real pain always seeps through the facade and punctures our mask, forcing us to look at ourselves. Or worse, reveal our truth sideways through bitterness and overcompensation.

I wasn't bitter about having my son, but I was bitter about the world I was bringing him into. I did not want the church world I could hardly understand to become a part of the village that would help me raise my son. The place I felt the least safe would now have access to my sweetest vulnerability, my baby boy.

I had to grow thick skin for the both of us.

Accepting that I would never fit in their roles, I attended church for direction from God, not affirmation from people. Simply put, when you have your baby at fourteen, you learn that you can't be too sensitive. You start telling yourself things before others can beat you to the punch. I assumed that everyone who knew my story was disappointed and pitied me. I didn't let that hurt me, though. I just decided not to care what people think.

Before having my son, all I cared about was what the people in my clique thought. I wanted to be seen as knowledgeable, beautiful, and cool. It was why I even started having sex. I wanted to make sure that I remained on the pedestal they placed me on, even if it was made of broken pieces and childish ideas of popularity.

If I didn't fit the mold before, how would I now, plus one, ever fit?

I had no intention of giving up. Idolizing successful women like Cathy Hughes and Oprah Winfrey, I dove into my schoolwork. Oprah had a son at fourteen. He passed away not long after his birth, though. Cathy Hughes had her son at sixteen. Both of them went on to create media empires. I kept their stories written in my heart. I had no clue how they got from point A to point B, but I wanted to try. Everyone else could think what they wanted about me. I was determined to prove "them" wrong. I would show them that I was so much more than just a single teen mom.

The people who felt I should be ejected from church and the outside world, like the girl in my high school, who questioned my intelligence, were wrong. I might be driving on a flat tire, but I would still get there. It may take me longer than it takes them, but I wouldn't stop. I had a plan and the heart to execute it. I didn't have time to search and see where my plan could fall apart. It simply had to work.

While I spent most days with a book in one hand and a baby bottle in the other, my sister enjoyed the freedom of being able to live in the moment. I lived vicariously through her. So when it was time for her sweet sixteen, I think I was more excited than she was. Cora and her friends gushed about dates, dresses, makeup, and more as they planned for her special birthday party.

"So about this date thing, is it mandatory?" I asked her after overhearing them one night.

"Of course," Cora giggled. "We'll find somebody for you."

I was so vested in completing my education that we had to ask around for a young man who'd be willing to escort me to my sister's party. It was just for one night, and then I could go back to focusing on what was important.

My sister's best friend, Brittney, said that her godbrother, Stephen, might be willing to come into town to go with me. After introducing our mothers and explaining the dilemma, we started talking on the phone. If we knew a little bit about each other, maybe the night wouldn't be so awkward. If Stephen ever judged me for having a child so early, I didn't know it. While we did continue talking long after the party was over, things eventually faded between us. The greatest gift he gave me was his sister. Each time I called to talk to him, his older sister, Stacia, and I would end up talking for hours.

Literally, there were times Stephen wouldn't even know I was on the phone. Eventually, I started calling just to talk to her. Stacia's daughter, Anastasia, was only a year older than Malachi. As teenaged mothers, we bonded over our desire to be better, but confessed to one another that we really didn't know where to start. It's ten years later, and the bond we shared has only strengthened. Stacia came to visit me in Texas so many times—a lot more than her brother ever did. We had sleepovers, laughed, cried, and made memories that we still smile about to this day. She's my sister.

I knew how much Stacia cared about me when it came time for my own sixteenth birthday. In order to reach my goal of graduating early, I had to attend summer school. So the summer I turned sixteen, I was taking chemistry and precalculus in a summer course. There were no plans for a sweet sixteen party for me. Among our friends, the tradition held that being a virgin was what made a "sweet sixteen." So I was fine without all the hoopla.

The day before my sixteenth birthday, however, I walked out of our small school building and looked for my ride. I assumed it would be my mom or one of my older brothers. But they were nowhere in sight. Instead, I saw someone motioning me toward a sleek black limo, definitely not what I was used to seeing in the high school carpool line.

Inside the limo Stacia and Stephen grinned back at me. My parents had planned a surprise birthday party for me. It was their way of showing me that they were still cheering for me. I didn't feel like I deserved the party, so I was never upset at the thought of not having one. I just didn't realize that when people love you, they pour hope into you. Love embraces who you are and inspires you to become better. So surrounded by my closest friends and family, I was being loved, in spite of my shortcomings. It made me want to excel even further. I wanted to make the people in that room so proud.

> *When people love you, they pour hope into you.*

With my newfound determination, I graduated two years after bringing my son into the world. He needed me and I needed his motivation.

In many ways, I guess you could say that the idea of not being able to ask for directions when we're lost (apparently not just men) applies to everyone at some point in life. Instead of pulling over and stopping completely, we continue to make turn after turn, hoping that one of them will put us back on the right track. From the outside looking in, it always appears that the lost person is too arrogant to admit they need help. The truth is, most of the time we have this feeling, this voice inside of us telling us that we're too close to give up. The voice makes us believe that we can do it, but it doesn't always mean we can do it alone.

How often do we get lost in life and never stop to ask God for His divine direction? Instead, we go to church each Sunday to receive more fuel to further our will, hardly ever asking what His will is for our lives. I prayed that God would help me live a life that proved those who doubted me wrong. I pleaded with Him to help me restore and rebuild my relationship with my family. I knew they loved me, but I wanted them to be proud of me. I prayed that God would help me make things right with others; I never asked Him how to make me right. I didn't think I was beyond repair, but I would have time to work on me after I made things right with them.

How often do we expect others to forgive us when we are incapable of forgiving ourselves? How do we teach others that we are worthy when we don't genuinely feel it? Our sin and shame become a filter that we believe the world sees us through, when really we just reflect onto people what we believe about ourselves.

Until we forgive ourselves, we will always see ourselves through the shattered pieces of the dreams we can no longer have. Nothing can be seen clearly through broken pieces: no future, no hope, no faith, no love is capable of being seen properly until we admit that we are driving on a flat tire. We have to stop believing that just because we are damaged we are irreparably broken.

Anything that breaks the structure of our hope must be repaired before daring to be whole again. Otherwise, we risk becoming susceptible to people's opinions, requiring their permission and acknowledgment to live and dream our own lives.

The human body experiences many pains in life. We can break our legs, nose, arms, fingers, and knees. We can bruise our ribs, liver, and shins. We can be broken over and over again, but we only experience death once.

The human spirit, on the other hand, is much more sensitive. One big disappointment, heartbreak, or misdirection and we stop living, even though we are far from dead. Instead of seeking the help we would for our body, we let our spirit remain broken, using the pain as a constant reminder of what happened and why it can never happen again.

Can you imagine a patient going to the emergency room with a broken leg, refusing the treatment that could heal him, and instead, asking for a wheelchair to make it through life? Sure he could make it, but why choose to stay broken? Somewhere along the way, I decided that remaining in motion was more important than taking the time to slow down and heal.

> *Instead of seeking the help we would for our body, we let our spirit remain broken.*

Long after the choir leaves the stand, the musicians put away their instruments, and the congregants have closed their Bibles, there is still you, your God, your doubt, and abundant grace. God is not asking us to be crucified for our sins—He sent His Son for that. He's asking us to make His sacrifice count. How can we honor Christ's life if we never explore the depths of His forgiveness or the beauty of grace?

I was about to find out.

4

Blueprint for the Future

LAST YEAR, TWO weeks before my twenty-fifth birthday, my family and I traveled to Australia. My father was due to minister at a very popular conference, called Hillsong, there in Sydney. Although it wasn't my first time traveling internationally, it was the farthest I had ever traveled from home. From Dallas, the trip to Australia is almost twenty hours.

Australia had always been one of my dream destinations. I heard so many stories about its beauty and wonderful people. More than that, I was incredibly excited to experience the Hillsong conference. My father, mother, and younger brother, Dexter, all spoke so highly of the worship experience. Words often failed them when describing the power they experienced at the gathering. In an arena with tens of thousands of people, there was such a unique opportunity to have an intimate encounter with God.

I did very little research leading up to the trip since I wanted to experience the country through fresh eyes. With the technology that exists, it's so easy to "travel" almost anywhere while hardly leaving your home. I suppose I could've planned my trip weeks before the plane touched down in the land Down Under, but I wanted to truly explore it for myself, meeting locals and asking for their recommendations about favorite aspects of their homeland. From quiet eateries to the sky lift at the zoo, I tried to see and learn as much as I could.

I learned quickly that there are many similarities between Australia and the States. Although there's no language barrier, since English is the primary language for both, words there are influenced by the Aussie culture and therefore have different meanings. Sometimes the strong accents and unique vernacular made it a bit more challenging to communicate than I'd anticipated.

For example, our first day out, I went to a local shop to purchase a few items I'd left behind. I was a bit concerned walking into the store that maybe the items would not be available, but fortunately I found exactly what I needed. After perusing the aisles for souvenirs and mementos to take home, I went to the register. The kind lady rang up my purchases, gave me the total, and I handed her my bank card. She swiped it, just like at home, and then asked me, "Charge or sign?"

I gave her a nervous smile and said, "Charge . . . ?"

I thought that's what I was supposed to say. To be honest, I couldn't be too sure what she meant. I assumed her question was the equivalent of asking if my transaction was credit or debit. She must've noticed my hesitation and decided to help me.

"Your number or no?" she said.

"Oh!" I exclaimed and quickly entered my PIN. Similar exchanges happened throughout the course of the trip. We were all speaking English, but the words had different meanings based on different cultural usage and context. On any occasion I went shopping during our time there (and I confess there were MANY), not once did anyone ever ask me, "Debit or credit?" I wasn't foolish enough to try to change or correct their term to fit what I knew. I recognized that I was in a new country, a new land, and therefore if I wanted an authentic experience, it would be necessary for me to learn to communicate their way.

During my senior year of high school, I wish I had made a commitment to understand myself with the same cultural curiosity I felt while in Australia. But I wasn't a very good tourist in my own country. As much as I tried to stay focused on motherhood and schoolwork, part of me longed to be carefree and focused on nothing more than going to the mall with friends. When prom time rolled around, I was surprised how much I longed to go.

Like most girls, I held the dream of attending prom as the closest to becoming Cinderella that you could imagine. Even if I did decide to attend, there was just one slight problem: I would never find a date. My son and my school were my primary focus. I wanted to go and have fun with friends, but I didn't want to be the only girl there who couldn't find a date. I didn't need a boyfriend, just a friend. I hoped I could find someone to share some laughs with friends and take a few pictures. Stephen, who had escorted me to Cora's sweet sixteen, now had a girlfriend, so he wasn't an option.

I'm naturally pretty shy, so there was no way that I would've approached anyone. It would've literally taken a miracle for my lips to separate enough for me to even broach the subject of asking someone to take me to prom. I shared my frustration with my mom. She understood the part of me that wanted to have a normal prom experience, but she also recognized that I couldn't risk any distractions.

However, she discreetly made it her mission to allow me an evening to just be a regular high school girl going to prom. After speaking to a few family friends, she found a friend from out of state who was willing to escort me to prom. He and I started conversing over the phone to ease the awkwardness of our first encounter, and he understood the importance of prom night for most girls my age.

Wanting me to enjoy my special night, my mother didn't explain to my date that my curfew had less to do with her and more to do with my baby-sitter. He had no idea I was a mother. We had a few conversations over the phone about general topics and interests, but I wasn't sure when I should explain to him my situation.

It was so easy to share the things I knew were great, but how do you share your vulnerability?

On one hand, our conversation was so normal. But there was an unspoken barrier between us that I didn't know how to overcome. It should have been quite simple, to just share my truth, but I couldn't get the whispers out of my head. How could I present the "new" me when everything else felt so incredibly familiar? I had no difficulty discussing how I managed to graduate early. Words never failed me when I spoke about my violin training or fluency in Spanish. It was so easy to share the things I knew were great, but how do you share your vulnerability?

How do you make yourself available to be embraced by others when you have yet to embrace yourself? So I fed myself a steady diet of negativity about others. Rather than risk judgment and rejection, I mostly isolated myself. Sometimes it's easier to call someone an enemy than to admit that you're afraid. When you choose to believe others can't handle your truth, you only give away the pieces of you that are universally acceptable—which only reinforces that other people can't handle the real you.

After I spent a couple weeks getting to know my prom date by phone, my mother asked me if I'd told him about Malachi. I told her I hadn't, and that I didn't know how. What would he think of me?

When I had my son, being a teen mom wouldn't get you instant stardom from a television show. When I was pregnant, there was no Facebook or Twitter to help spread the news. You could find some information on the Internet, but a lot of it was subjective and speculative. It would be up to me to tell my truth. I was afraid, though. I didn't think it was possible for someone to not prejudge me for becoming a mother before I could even drive a car.

I was very proud of the work I was doing to create a better tomorrow for my son and me, but I didn't want to be judged until my process was over. I just didn't want that to be the end of our story. The old whispers about girls who had gotten pregnant at a young age echoed in my mind. People shook their heads and talked about how their lives would be ruined forever. No matter how much good they had done before their pregnancy, or what they attempted afterward, it was apparently all inconsequential.

I figured that someday I would present my story when I was finished making it pretty. Someday I would proudly announce that I was a teen mom and that I had gone on to become successful despite what others said I could not do. I just wasn't there yet. I was still building.

Before any construction can begin, an architect draws a picture of what will be the completed structure. It is by this guide that they determine what supplies they will need, how long the process will take, and the labor required to transform the picture into a building. In my mind I knew what I wanted my life to look like. I had mapped everything out and estimated how long it would take me to get there. At the time, however, I didn't realize that nothing, including my idea of a perfect life, would just appear by itself.

Construction doesn't just require time; it makes quite a bit of noise. No matter how much we would like to work on ourselves quietly, sometimes we can't avoid calling attention to ourselves. No more than you can stop the clang of a hammer or the buzz of a saw can you hide the pieces of your life necessary to become whole. We want to be under construction, but we don't want to be noticed in the midst of our growing pains.

Construction doesn't just require time; it makes quite a bit of noise. No matter how much we would like to work on ourselves quietly, sometimes we can't avoid calling attention to ourselves.

How do we embrace the process of not having it all together? How can we allow ourselves to make the noise necessary to construct our new life?

I had the plan in my mind, and I was acquiring the tools necessary to put everything together, but I was yet under construction. Telling my story so early would risk exposing others to my building process. I would be asking them to look at the wood, the paint, the nails, the shovels, and the glass and see a finished structure.

It's not always easy to trust others' eyes to see your dream the way you see it. When you're under construction, everyone becomes an architect. They want to rearrange your dream to fit what they think it should look like or what they believe is more attainable. They say things like, "Don't dream so big!" and "You can do better," or, worse, "You'll never build a life like that."

It's not always easy to trust others' eyes to see your dream the way you see it. When you're under construction, everyone becomes an architect.

I kept my son a secret not because I wasn't proud of him but because I was trying to protect him from those who wouldn't see his life, or mine, the way I did. You can't grow by hiding, though, so I finally told my prom date about my son. I explained to him that I was excelling in school and applying to the best universities within driving distance because underneath it all there was a young, precious life that was my foundation. My son was keeping me grounded so that I could build something stronger than shame, prejudice, or fear.

After a few polite questions, our conversation basically returned to normal. In that moment I realized that my goal shouldn't be helping others to see that a teen mother can go on to be great. The best thing for me to do is to accept the direction of my life and dare to let that acceptance flow to others.

The most important part of any building, person, or plan is the foundation. No matter how well the framing is done, electricity wired, plumbing installed, or fixtures selected, if the foundation is weak, nothing can stand. The foundation is the least visible but the most necessary.

Who are you at the core of your being?

Outside of your education, finances, occupation, or achievements, underneath all the material things that the world can see, what makes you get up in the morning?

What do you tell yourself about your destiny in the stillness of night?

I had a foundation, but it was built on wanting people to accept me, not my accepting myself. I continued building until I graduated with my diploma at sixteen. I applied to college after college so that I could add a degree to the materials with which I was constructing my life. Because of my age and the fact that I couldn't stay on campus like most freshmen because of my son, it was not easy finding a university that would be flexible with my situation. Finally, I was accepted to Texas Christian University, less than thirty minutes from home. Since I didn't have my driver's license yet, my mother or another relative or family friend would have to drive me to school.

I was excited about beginning my college career at a school like TCU. My siblings and I had been homeschooled in the years leading to my pregnancy. Then my parents placed us in a private school where we could interact socially but still remain focused on our schooling. My senior class had twenty-one students in it. My sister and I were the only African Americans in the entire school. Outside of church, it was very rare for us to be in a social setting where we were not the only blacks. So while others at TCU complained about the lack of diversity, I was excited to have a "normal" experience.

The most important part of any building, person, or plan is the foundation. The foundation is the least visible but the most necessary.

I decided to study accounting, but first I would have to get into the business school. My college education was a pivotal part of my plan. I wanted to become an accountant and eventually become chief financial officer for the church. What better way to complete the process of forgiveness than to be trained to help my dad? When I first shared my plans, my parents were both so excited. I led them to believe that it was what I truly wanted, because I didn't want them to know I was still seeking their forgiveness.

My first day in college, I packed my backpack, found a cute outfit, and waited for my mom to get ready to drop Malachi off at day care and then me off to college. I was hoping that since my class was still in the morning, not many people would see my mother dropping me off. Let's face it, having a chauffeur is nice, but not when it's your mother and not when you're in college!

Nervous wasn't even the word for it.

After turning seventeen over the summer, here I was on a college campus. A part of me felt like everything might end up being okay. I remember thinking, *Perhaps I really can pull this off: become successful and care for my child in a way that makes both of us better people.*

I got to campus about fifteen minutes before my class was scheduled to begin so that I could navigate the building where my class would be held. Discreetly reaching for my map, I tried to find my way to Beasley Hall.

My first course for the day was communications; it was a diverse class with a mix of students from across the country. As far as diversity goes, there seemed to be a lot of it. Even though there was only one other black female, my class was about 40 percent black. I overheard that the guys in the class with me were football players. I sat quietly in the back of the classroom, trying to keep to myself.

Danielle, the other black girl in the class, was the first to speak to me. We became fast friends and created a bit of a ritual. We'd go to class, then walk together to the student union until our next class began. She knew some of the football players and would speak to them after class when they gathered on the steps of Beasley.

I'd usually stand to the side while she playfully interacted with them, waiting for her to catch up with them so we could walk to the other side of campus. One day while waiting on her, I started chatting with one of the players, Robert. Over the course of the semester while Danielle was catching up with some of the friends she'd made on the team, Robert and I would talk for a few minutes. Flirtatious banter and jokes soon became our "thing."

We eventually exchanged numbers and started texting occasionally. Then we had our first telephone conversation and everything changed. He seemed terribly obnoxious and arrogant over the phone. He called once more before I decided we had nothing to talk about.

Overall, my first semester at TCU was pretty normal. Soon I met a nice guy named Deon, delved into my schoolwork during the day, cared for Malachi in the evening, and did homework at night. I was finding a rhythm. Outside of Danielle and a few other juniors and seniors, I didn't have many friends my own age. I didn't live on campus, and I was only there for my classes, so I didn't really have a way to become socially involved. I usually walked from class to class alone. It seemed like my plan was going according to schedule. Nonetheless, I still felt anxious, as if waiting for some other shoe to drop.

> *Sometimes we can be so unfamiliar with peace that we do whatever we can to jeopardize it.*

There are these moments, these quiet times, in our life when it seems like just for a moment everything will be okay. Then we become afraid that the moment is too good to be true, so we don't rest in those times. Sometimes we can be so unfamiliar with peace that we do whatever we can to jeopardize it. How tragic is it when we are only comfortable when we are surrounded by discomfort? I had found as much peace as I could with my journey, but I was still hoping to show my family, my church, and the world I could recover.

I didn't speak much to anyone on campus. Sure, news had spread that T.D. Jakes's daughter was attending the school, but no one knew my story or could easily recognize my face. I liked it that way. I didn't want to draw any more interest to myself than necessary. By spring semester, I finally had my driver's license, which helped me become more involved on campus and meet a few more friends. My routine was pretty much the same: go to class, hang out in the student union, pick up Malachi from day care, study, and take care of Chi in the evening. My friendly courtship with Deon was coming to an end, which was fine.

Our relationship had been casual and friendly, but we were looking for such different things at that time in our lives. He was older and more mature, ready to settle down. I knew that I needed to focus and couldn't afford many distractions. Toward the end of my first year at Texas Christian University, I had not changed much. I was still very focused and committed to making a better future for my son and myself.

A few weeks after Deon and I broke up, I ran into Robert, and we soon resumed our casual, flirtatious banter. It was not without second thoughts, though, because I remembered how obnoxious he'd been on the phone. Danielle had also warned me back then that Robert—like many of the other football players—was bad news. He had a reputation for being strong-willed, overly confident, and a bit unruly. On the playing field these traits made him an exceptional leader and passionate motivator, the same qualities that attracted me.

I knew firsthand what it was like to have a lot of people think negatively about you, and I wanted to form my own opinion about Robert. Despite that arrogant alpha routine on the phone shortly after we first met, I wanted to give him a fair chance. When you become the victim of rumors and prejudgment, you become more compassionate when you hear someone else being judged. I chose to ignore what everyone said about Robert because one day I wanted everyone to ignore what they heard about me. I chose to give him the chance that I wanted others to give me.

And he surprised me. There was something vulnerable within his strength, something tender and fragile. So we began talking . . . and talking . . . for hours. In between classes, while sitting in the car outside the dorm, or on the phone before bed, we talked and grew closer.

Outside of what everyone thought about him, he was actually a very funny and charming person. I felt fortunate that I was able to see a side of him that others didn't get to see. We were a lot alike: a reputation that preceded us but a heart at its core that was beautiful and willing to give and receive love anyway.

I started to love the broken pieces in him that looked so much like my own jagged edges. And besides, we weren't in a relationship, just good friends. On Easter, I invited him over for our family's annual party. It was the first time he would see the other side of my world.

After spending most of the holiday together laughing, eating, and joking around, I drove him back to the campus dorms. We had two completely different backgrounds, yet we had this universal commonality: We were broken. He told me about his daughter and her sister that he was also caring for. I told him about my son, which actually took some time convincing him was true. He had heard of my dad but didn't really think that it was as big of a deal as others on campus made it to be. Robert never asked me to get a book signed for his mother or to schedule a time for him to meet with my dad for prayer.

I liked that. I liked that he didn't care who I was or that I had a son. For the first time in my life, it seemed like all someone wanted from me was me.

Most guys that I dated were afraid of my father. Between his appearance (over six-foot-four) and his occupation, my dad was a daunting presence for any potential boyfriends.

No one ever dared to get on his bad side. Our friends used to joke that getting in trouble with our dad would also get you in trouble with God. It started off pretty funny, but when you see your dad as just your dad, it starts to get old. Robert was the first person who dared to not care about what my dad did. I was attracted to that in him. I had been so busy trying to earn my father's respect, maintain his forgiveness, and make him proud that the idea of emulating Robert's nonchalant attitude was very appealing.

I still didn't feel like I had any place in church, and with the difficulty of my courses increasing, I started to question whether my plan to become CFO was even feasible. The idea of changing my major, though, after talking for almost a year about how much help I could offer the ministry, would go directly against everything I had told my friends and family. I didn't want to seem indecisive or, worse, risk disappointing them again. I didn't feel like I had much room for any more errors.

I wanted to be more like Robert.

I made decisions for my life based on how I thought others felt. I never checked to actually see if what I thought was fact. Trapped between a rock and a hard place, I let Robert become my escape. I wanted to borrow from his strength; I just didn't know that it would mean I had to give mine away.

Fear has got to be one of the greatest emotions humans experience. We depend on its strength to teach unforgettable lessons. We hope that the fear of getting burned will be enough to keep us from touching fire. I was afraid of disappointing my family. I felt like life hadn't left me with many other opportunities to mess up. I put the pressure on myself, but it was easier to think it was what everyone expected from me. I needed the pressure to motivate me because I didn't have time to find my passion. Robert had all of this passion and seemed so immune to pressure.

He expected nothing from me and I appreciated that, because it was easier than having to admit that I was afraid of failing. It is, in my opinion, the same reason why the cliché that misery loves company rings so true. When you are surrounded by happy people, they expect you to be happy. Miserable people don't expect you to be anything other than miserable.

When two people are broken when they meet, like Robert and I were, they aren't looking for someone to make them better. They just want to connect with someone who doesn't expect them to be anything other than broken. Sure, I had plans on healing, and maybe, if I was strong enough, I could help him heal, too. But right then, in the moment, I didn't want our relationship to be anything other than two broken people searching for the bridge to healing.

We both had the same goal of outrunning our pasts and creating a better future. So we bonded over our dreams, pain, fear, and disappointment. I knew his reputation, but I knew mine, too. I didn't care what others thought about him because I knew what those people would say about me.

A week before the semester ended, I called Robert to see if we could hang out. He told me that he couldn't because he was packing to move out of his dorm . . .

. . . and into an apartment with his fiancée.

5

Complications

I SHOULD'VE BACKED away.

"Your fiancée?" I asked, trying not to lose it.

"It's sort of complicated," Robert said. "She'll deal, you'll see."

Between my friend Danielle's warnings and Robert's abrupt decision to move into an apartment with a fiancée he had never once mentioned, I should've run and never looked back. Instead, I continued to see him as if nothing had happened. I was dating an engaged man. I thought that if I played the supportive friend role, he would see that I was the one he should be with. I made a conscious decision, and hurt another woman in order to pursue a man who could not see my worth, regardless of how much of me I gave him.

I've pondered whether or not to fully admit this truth to the world because it would've been so easy to just play the victim. I could say that I was a good girl who did all the right things, gave my all to my dream man, only to end up devastated. However, I know the truth and recognize my part in what happened. I know with certainty that such a story is too real for so many women. And I could never diminish their pain to protect my name.

I also know that my story is not unique. For quite a few women who are broken and ashamed, like I've been, we actively play a role in hurting another woman just so a man can validate us. Piece by piece we give ourselves away, hoping that each piece will amount to enough to make us special to him. Whether it's our finances, our bodies, our ideas, or our reputations, we find ourselves giving everything we have away.

Eventually we settle and begin to believe that maybe this is the best that life has to offer us. We hear horror story after horror story of relationships gone awry, and we decide that the whole world is settling so we might as well, too. Somewhere along the way we lose the belief in fairy tales, let alone mature love, and settle for something we'd never wish for our own daughters, yet somehow become content to have for ourselves.

It's not to say that a relationship with the right person doesn't take a lot of work. While I am certainly no expert on love or relationships, I believe that marriage with the right person is worth the investment. I still believe in the kind of love and marriage that has more good days than bad. I still believe that marriage is supposed to be a reflection of Christ's love for the church. And marriage, like the church, becomes more complicated when you begin intermixing different opinions and personalities. But still, despite life's complicated dynamics, I believe that with both church and marriage it's possible to have more love than fear.

To this day, when I look back on the beginning stages of heartbreak with Robert and how early in our courtship it was, I have to soul search to discover how I gave up on my dream of love so quickly. If I'm honest with myself, it was my insecurity. Part of me had quietly grieved that another could never fully accept my situation. Robert was the first guy who, when I told him about my son, didn't let it affect how he felt about me, and a part of me swooned. I didn't think anyone could so easily accept that I had a child so early on in my life.

Robert, a linebacker for our university's football team, was popular around campus and appeared so comfortable in his own skin. His indifference to my father's status was, at the time, attractive. Although now I view his attitude as a warning, then it seemed like a relief. He was the first person who didn't elevate me to some heavenly pedestal. Still, I grieve the fact that my insecurity didn't injure just me. Unintentionally, I inflicted wounds on so many others. I allowed myself not only to be degraded but to degrade others because I decided he was more important than their hearts.

I take ownership for those wounds.

I apologize for every text, call, date, kiss, and other selfish acts committed to feed my own insecurity. My self-doubt made me an assailant. And in these decisions I reaped everything I sowed.

No matter how well things look on the outside, until you confront your wrongs, you cannot create rights.

When I first began the journey of healing from my heartbreak, a part of me was bitter. I felt like the women he used to hurt me went on to live happy lives while I suffered picking up the pieces. Since then, I've learned the "other woman" never gets away. No matter how well things look on the outside, until you confront your wrongs, you cannot create rights. There is no honor in betrayal. I couldn't share honestly about my life now without acknowledging the role I played in my own heartbreak and that of other women.

It would be so easy to say I was young. It would be even easier to say, like many do, that I had no responsibility at all because I never made a commitment to his fiancée. After having had the bitter taste of my own medicine, though, I now see that you cannot desire trust and sow betrayal.

When he told me he was moving in with his fiancée, my heart imploded. I tried to hush the internal voice that told me the rumors were right about him and that I should just cut my losses. At the very least, I wanted some answers. I wanted to know how he could've made me feel so special and then just walk away like I was nothing. Without seeing my relationship with him clearly and objectively, I was dangerously close to feeling like I would never recover. All my hope had shifted to getting his affirmation; he had become my savior. I believed that I knew and understood him like no one else. We had something different and more special than what he had with his fiancée—or anyone else.

He reinforced this odd kind of relational purgatory. He told his fiancée that he and I were friends and that she would have to adjust. I didn't care whether she liked it or not, as long as I could be around him.

Most of the athletes at TCU had to enroll in summer classes to stay on course with their degree programs. My parents had a very strict either-school-or-work policy, so I enrolled in courses over the summer to spend time with Robert, work toward my degree, and take care of Chi in the evening.

After going to summer school in order to graduate early from high school, I felt like I could handle the responsibility. In hindsight I realize how childish it was to juggle a dysfunctional relationship, college-level summer courses, and a growing toddler. I felt like I could do it, though.

How often do we add burden after burden, then complain about the weight of it all?

My mornings started with taking Malachi to day care, "carpooling with friends" (picking up Robert for class), and then spending every possible minute with Robert until I had to get my son. Even if it meant sitting in the bleachers and reading while Robert worked out on the field with his teammates, I was almost always with him. It became our routine. Occasionally he would mention how our "friendship" made his fiancée insecure, and I would allow the convicted part of me to speak.

"Well, maybe we shouldn't talk anymore," I would say, "or maybe I should just see you less."

"No, I don't think that's necessary," he'd say. "You're too important to me. I can't lose you."

"I don't want to come between you, though."

"She'll handle it, no big deal. You know how special you are to me, don't you?"

His words fed my insecurity until my conscience finally had to quiet down.

Every day from early May to the end of the first summer session at the end of June, I saw Robert. He was all I wanted to know. I can't even remember the classes I took—and failed— that summer. But I can tell you the songs we listened to in the car on the way to class or the way he celebrated an interception in practice.

The idea of our becoming something and proving others wrong about our pasts was too appealing to me. I would be his Bonnie and he would be my Clyde. Sure, our situation wasn't perfect, but it was *ours*, something we shared.

> *Like a tool, love should be used to build something incredible, not to destroy fragile material.*

Now I see that love should be used as a tool, not a weapon. Like a tool, love should be used to build something incredible, not to destroy fragile material.

The wedding was off.

My relationship with Robert would no longer be creating a dilemma for any of us.

He was moving out and breaking the engagement. Whether the split was a result of his leaving or her asking him to go, I never found out, but I was glad. I had finally won and would have one less thing to feel guilty about. Finally, he and I could just be together. With no complications.

The day Robert got the keys to his new apartment, I wanted him to see he had made the right decision. I would have his back and he would never miss his former fiancée again. I cleaned his new place from top to bottom, then decorated it to make him more comfortable. Using what money I had from tutoring middle school students, my savings, and the charge card for the university bookstore, I tried to create a home for him.

While my parents knew we were dating, they had no idea exactly how much time we were spending together. They assumed, because I led them to believe, that school was completely under control and I was just casually dating Robert, much like I had done with Deon.

I knew they would never approve of such a huge distraction at such a pivotal moment in my life. I also knew that when a person wants something badly enough, she'll do whatever it takes to get it. Throwing all I had into this dance with Robert, I didn't want my parents to know how cheaply I had placed myself on sale. So I quietly placed my self-esteem on the clearance rack while I tried to earn enough validation to be whole.

I've always wanted to meet that person who flees when the first red flag is waved. There's no doubt what I would have told my closest friend to do if she were in the same situation in which I had now entangled myself. But I wanted to believe so badly that our relationship would work. So I convinced myself that warning signs were merely complications to be overcome, red curtains blocking our view rather than exclamations of imminent danger.

Although our routine remained the same once Robert moved out of his fiancée's home, we made the decision not to rush into anything. We would just remain friends. We knew that getting involved in a serious committed relationship so quickly would only confirm his fiancée's fears. There was no need to rush, anyway; we had created a great friendship, and anything further would be well worth the wait.

As the summer came to an end, Robert started two-a-day football practices, which allowed me to focus on the things I'd let slide while chasing his love. Training camp was so grueling that we didn't get to talk as much as we once did. We'd talk briefly whenever he could take a break, but not like it had been earlier in the summer. I missed him, but I really had a lot of work to make up. By the time camp came to an end, I was all caught up and actually balancing work, parenting, and our friendship.

> *I convinced myself that warning signs were merely complications to be overcome, red curtains blocking our view rather than exclamations of imminent danger.*

I enrolled in my classes for my sophomore year promising to be more dedicated and committed than before. And I wouldn't have much of a choice either; my parents were investing in me, not sending me to school to audition for *The Bachelorette*. I could hear their voices in my head so clearly.

"We're so proud of you, Sarah."

"You're really working hard and that's what it takes."

"Keep going, girl!"

"We will invest in your goals as long as you invest your efforts at the same level."

They assumed the best about me, and I didn't want to give them any evidence that the worst was yet to come. In fact, I had no idea myself.

One night a couple weeks into my sophomore year, I was home studying but finally couldn't resist checking in on Facebook. Due to that obnoxious phone conversation not long after we first met, Robert and I had never become friends on Facebook. And we didn't need to since we talked almost every day.

And at this point, I had too much pride to add him as a friend after making such a big deal out of ignoring his initial request. This didn't prevent me from stalking his page from time to time, though. So periodically I would type in each letter of his name and smile.

That September evening was not much different, except this time when Robert's profile finished loading, there were photos of him, his ex-girlfriend—the one he dated *before* his fiancée—and her friends in the apartment I had vacuumed and cleaned for him just days before. Apparently, his ex was now his ex-ex. Within seconds I was breathing fire. Livid is an understatement. I had sacrificed my time, money, heart, and morals. And he was throwing it all right back in my Facebook.

I had too much pride

to admit

that I had gambled

on love and lost.

Now, before I continue and share what happened that night, I know you've got to be wondering why my relationship with Robert didn't end right there. What could compel me to stay when it was so clear that our relationship was in trouble? As I look back, the truth stares back at me, not accusingly but compassionate and clear-eyed.

The truth is, I had too much pride to admit that I had gambled on love and lost. From a young age, girls hear these stories about love making someone better. Somehow I thought that if I was good enough to him, then he would want to be good to me, too. Isn't that how relationships are supposed to work?

I grew up watching my mother care for my father. She never raised her voice, constantly kept a clean home, made his plates, and ran his bath water. He provided for her, listened to her, encouraged her, served her, and surprised her with little notes, presents, and special dates. I had no definition of what a loving relationship was like outside of their commitment. Looking back, I realize now that long before marriage was on the table, I had given myself to the role of Robert's wife, even though I would cry many more tears before I ever became one.

Sure, I told myself, he was a little rough around the edges, but who isn't? Even if those edges were sharp, I had given too much of myself away to turn back. The personal investment was too great to lose without a return. What if no one else would ever accept my truth the way he did? What if no one else would understand the pressure of being T.D. Jakes's daughter? Or how badly I just wanted to be me? Who else could I bare that truth to?

The older I've gotten, the more I've realized I'm not alone in feeling this way. Although I felt like an anomaly, almost every woman I've met has had a relationship where she wishes she had held back more so she didn't have to walk away with so much less. We're all human.

Out of our insecurities we determine our needs. The person who doesn't feel beautiful wants to think that she is, so we do anything for the person who makes us have that feeling, even if it's fleeting. This is shaky ground. The difficulty of a relationship increases dramatically when it's built on a deficiency. It's like a vitamin deficiency, where you can eat every day and never notice what your body is missing until months into the problem.

I knew I was lost with Robert, but I didn't know that I was in trouble. But it didn't matter because I would have done anything to ease the constant reminder of my deficiency. I wanted to be enough, and not just for Robert. I wanted to be enough for Malachi, my dad, my mother, and my friends.

The things that I did to prove my worth—cooking, cleaning, helping with papers, and being a chauffeur—were all desperate attempts to get him to tell me I was enough. And somehow, despite the injuries to my ego, Robert rewarded me. He had the ability to make me feel I was enough, at least for that moment.

The difficulty of a relationship increases dramatically when it's built on a deficiency.

But such hindsight only comes with time. In that moment when I saw him, his former girlfriend, and her friends sitting in his apartment, I felt like their fingers were wrapped around my hope, determined to choke the life from it. I only had one thought: If I wasn't enough, nothing I brought to the table would be enough, either. After seeing the photos, I quickly looked at the time. It was still pretty early in the evening, so I knew Robert had gone from practice to mandatory tutoring. I would have about two hours to use my spare key and empty out his apartment.

Since it suddenly seemed clear that I was going to lose in my attempts to win him over, I could at least try and take back as much as I could. I called some of the guys I knew on campus, mostly Robert's teammates, and told them what happened. With my angry sister by my side and my son safely with my aunt, I made the drive to open the apartment and let the guys in. Within thirty minutes everything was gone.

I decided I would rather give the stuff to the guys helping me than have Robert and Ms. Double Ex make it their running joke. I felt like Robert had merely used me until she came home from visiting her family during the summer. Being angry was so much easier than admitting to being hurt, or worse, even lost. I hated her. I hated that I wasn't her, and more than that, I hated that I wanted to be her. I hated that Robert didn't forsake her for me and that when it came down to who was going to be hurt, me or her, I was chosen to bleed.

I didn't realize that winning him would mean losing me. I had given so much of myself to him that losing him somehow felt worse than losing what little of me I had left. But in the heat of my anger that night, I felt vindicated. I had done what I could to make my message clear. Loud and clear.

Sure enough, once Robert returned home to his empty apartment, he knew I was the culprit. He called me enraged. Yelling at the top of his lungs, calling me every name in the book, he was upset because I had betrayed him. He was wrong, though. I hadn't betrayed him. The cause of this mess was that I trusted him.

When he finished hurling every curse word in the book at me, he explained why he was so upset. In those first few months in his new apartment, he had felt like he had a home, more than ever before in his life. Now I had taken away that level of security he had always longed for and only recently found.

But I didn't care.

It wasn't enough for me, because he couldn't see what I lost. He couldn't see what I sacrificed on the altar of our love only to see it thrown aside without so much as a call. He would be all right. He and his former flame and all their friends could sleep on the floor for all I cared. I hung up, turned my phone off, and went to bed.

But it was far from over.

The next morning I woke up to a call from his coach. If I didn't get the "gifts" back to Robert within twenty-four hours, they were calling the police. Talk about the last thing I needed to happen! If my parents ever found out, there would be nothing anyone could do to save me. I'd have to drop out of school and my whole dream of working at the church someday would dissolve.

So I got dressed as soon as I could and started calling the guys who had helped me the night before. A few told me I was on my own, while a couple offered to help move what they could. Soon chipped plates, dirty towels, an incomplete silverware set, and dozens of other items were returned in the worst possible condition.

Between the haste of the move and the frustration of their involvement, I wasn't expecting stellar moving services. I apologized to Robert in front of his coach and headed home for the evening, defeated. Less than twenty-four hours before, I had felt completely justified; now I was just hoping that I could live this down on campus.

The incident with Robert was a momentary wake-up call. When I was on campus, wasn't I supposed to be getting an education instead of a reputation? It wasn't that I didn't want to learn, but simply that I wanted time with Robert more.

On those rare occasions when I wasn't skipping class with him or avoiding test days, I did okay. I had tried to keep up, but there were at least two classes that even if I aced every assignment from that point forward, I would still fail. So I did all that I could to preserve the remaining three classes. With some focus and dedicated effort, I could get at least a B in each of them.

With a renewed commitment to my future, I immediately fell off the scene. I went to class. I went home. I didn't want to see anyone who could have known about the apartment situation. I started making some headway in those classes. I even managed to put my phone down for hours at a time just so that I could play with Malachi. I showed my face at family functions more and even made it to church. I was finding my way back. Glimpses of who I used to be made me realize how far away I'd gotten.

Glimpses of who I used to be made me realize how far away I'd gotten.

And then Robert called.

"Sarah, it's me," he said. "Don't hang up."

"What is it?" I tried to sound tough, businesslike.

"I broke up with her. When I saw how much it hurt you, I just couldn't stand the thought of you in so much pain. I'm . . . I'm sorry, baby. I told her that I don't ever want to see her again, that we can't even be friends."

"Yeah, right," I said, amazed at his ability to say all the right things.

"I wish you had let me explain the pictures on Facebook before you pulled your little stunt," he said. "It was no big thing. We were just chillin' and joking around. She didn't mean anything to me, just an old friend, you know."

"What do you expect me to say?" My voice cracked just like my defenses.

"I understand why you did what you did, though," he said and chuckled. "I didn't realize you cared so much."

"Well, I shouldn't have," I said.

"It's okay, kinda makes me feel special."

Nothing but static on the line and tears in my eyes.

"Sarah," he said, and his voice got softer, "I really miss you."

Torn between a love that made me lose myself and a God who made me confront the truth I didn't want to see, I chose Robert. I told myself I had time to better my relationship with God. Lots of time—the rest of my life. But I had already lost Robert and now could have him back. I didn't want to lose him again. So I was willing to do whatever it took.

Including making his now ex my worst enemy. Robert and I could rebuild what was broken, but not with her around. That's how you defend making the third party more important than the one you're with. So I tore her down in any way I could. Tried to attack her with our differences and taunt her with moments he and I had spent together. I tried to break her because I was broken. I wanted to leave her with the same bitter taste that I had.

And she played back. She would tell me that he was only using me for money. Or that when I had to leave to go take care of Malachi they spent their night playing house. These games went on for months. After football games we would stand on opposite sides of the players' exit. I imagine her heart, like mine, was in her chest each game, hoping as I was that she had done enough this week to earn the coveted place beside him.

Too oblivious (or too obsessed) to care what anyone else thought, we were both his willing pawns. We were eager, ready, and available at his whim. Once again, Robert was my only focus. When I got home I had my son, but I was on the phone or rushing through our routine so that I could keep my preoccupation with the only person I thought had the power to validate me.

I had given myself away and lost him. Now I'd gotten him back and was determined to fight so that I'd never lose him again.

I still had no idea that it was a battle I could never win.

6

Constellations

IN GRADE SCHOOL when it was time to learn about constellations, I dreaded every moment of it. In fact, when I enrolled at Texas Christian University and learned that one of the core science class options was astronomy, I immediately enrolled in sociology. I was never able to see the constellations in the sky. Even on the clearest of nights, as beautiful as the stars were, they just looked like stars to me.

The ability to look up into the sky and see the Big Dipper, Little Dipper, or Orion's Belt would have seriously filled in some of the gaps in my childhood. I always felt so dumb when others could see them but I couldn't. I truly did want to see the formations in the sky, and I got away with pretending. I'd nod my head, ooh and ahh, then direct the attention back to ground level.

Several years and many tears after that fateful phone call from Robert, I stepped out onto the porch of my home and sat on the front steps. This summer evening was such a nice break from the usual scorching temperatures of Dallas. Every few minutes the wind would blow and the summer breeze danced across my face. I don't think I'd ever felt so much peace in my life. Finally, I reluctantly stood; it was time for me to prepare for bed. But not before I took one last moment to catch a few more of the sweet summer drafts that had me in such a daze. I closed my eyes to take in the beauty of the moment. When I opened my eyes to the dark night sky, I saw it.

The Big Dipper.

Without even trying, I could see it clearly. It was as if it had been waiting there the entire time for me to see it. I wondered if it was just the area or the weather conditions or seasonal atmosphere that were more conducive to my seeing it. On the other hand, I think that maybe it was just the season of my life I was in.

After years and years of trying to force the stars in my life to align, I had given up. I had stopped trying to make people be who I wanted them to be in life. I had released people from the roles I wanted them to play in my life and instead let them define themselves. Just like the stars, everyone in my life had fallen into their divine design. I could see clearer than ever what God was trying to show me all along.

Each time I looked for a constellation in the past, I tried to force stars that didn't belong into the picture. Silly, huh? How could I want things or people to just be who they are, but rush the process before they could truly show themselves?

Oddly enough, the realization that I could've seen the Big Dipper thousands of times before that moment didn't bother me. I know that it probably should have, but there was something about the picture coming together when I least expected it that outweighed the lost time. My life was so drastically different between then and now. I felt like I had finally found my place in the world.

Maybe all this time God has been waiting for the stars to align in my life so that I could see how beautiful things can be made with dangerous material. As beautiful as the bright twinkles in the sky are, they're made of the most volatile combination of hydrogen and helium. In their simplest form, stars are explosions of energy. Isn't it incredible that something so dangerous up close serves as one of the most reliable tools for navigation when seen from a distance? As a matter of fact, if you can find the Big Dipper, it is so much easier to find the North Star.

These little explosions that we could never touch or fully understand help us find our way. To the rest of the world the star is beautiful, but the star knows the truth. It knows that some beauty can only come from the process of combining the things that threatened to harm us.

I wanted Robert to be my North Star.

Sure, it was dangerous, but I could keep enough of my heart away to not get burned. He felt like the missing piece to my puzzle. If we could turn all of our fire, passion, and energy into a star, then maybe it would right all the things we thought needed fixing. Maybe our love would create a light so bright that neither of us had to be lost again. We could just depend on one another to create something dazzling, something that would help us find our way.

After our phone call, the one where he said all the right things and apologized and told me about breaking up with his "friend," I gathered the bits and pieces of my heart, hope, and self-esteem and poured them into him. I knew that being with me meant taunting in the locker room about the girl who had his apartment cleared out. I could only imagine what kind of ridicule he would face. Although, to this day I think that many of his teammates understood that every action has a reaction. Still, I saw his willingness to undergo that level of ego-bruising as a sign that we were willing to take risks on each other.

Finally, after months of going back and forth, he was actually taking a chance on me, too. It crossed my mind that maybe she was just finished with him and I had "won" him by default. But sometimes you have to choose between a scorned heart and a lying tongue.

I wish I could've seen choosing to protect myself as a viable option. What if I didn't have to choose between trusting him or her and just left the entire situation alone? I could still stay low-key. I really didn't have a big community of friends on campus. The ones I might have had either picked sides with Robert's exes or didn't want to be associated with my drama. And who could blame them?

To this day, Brittany, one of my dear friends who was at TCU with us, still laughs when she sees me. Although we knew each other then, we really only became close after our TCU days. Brittany always laughed at me for bringing my designer bag to football games. She had no idea I had more fake bags than real ones. We still laugh about the day I dropped my bag on the ground after a football game.

I wish I could've seen choosing to protect myself as a viable option.

Outside of my own roller-coaster romance with Robert, other players on the team juggled groupies, ex-girlfriends, friends, and even wives—and many of us waited outside the locker room for the players to exit after a game. Most of the time it was easier to look like you weren't trying at all than to wait at the front of the crowd with bated breath. Waiting on Robert became a war between me and whichever ex-girlfriend he was claiming to be "friends" with at the moment. After one game, Brittany was waiting with me. I saw Robert's ex-girlfriend—the one whose pictures I'd seen on Facebook—standing on the opposite side of the door. The players came out one by one at first, but then several at a time. Robert came out with a few of his friends, and then I lost his head in the crowd. When the people finally dispersed, there he was walking toward the dorms with his ex-girlfriend. Before I knew it, I was walking toward them at a rapid pace.

When I finally caught up to them, I dropped my purse, took my jewelry off, and prepared to brawl. In the middle of it all, I heard Brittany yell, "GIRL, PICK UP THAT PURSE. IT COSTS TOO MUCH MONEY!"

We laugh about it now, but I was too furious to laugh then. I'm not proud of it, but that's all I knew to do in the moment. At heart I knew that fighting her wouldn't fix anything, but I was tired of the back-and-forth.

He was mine, yet here he was walking away after the game with his ex-girlfriend? The dynamic had shifted yet again, but I wouldn't be defeated. If the two of them were just friends, then we could all be friends. Somehow what should have been an issue between me and Robert became a battle between me and his ex. She was the new competition and he was the judge. I was intent on showing them both that I was confident enough to withstand their friendship.

Another piece of me went on sale, marked down for final clearance.

And with that, another piece of me went on sale, marked down for final clearance.

I was too afraid to be honest, so I chose to live a lie. I was willing to play a game that would risk my facade becoming my painful reality. I wish I had been brave enough to admit that I was weak. Some months later into my relationship with Robert, I heard the saying, "You teach people how to treat you." While I understood the basic fundamentals of that theory, I had taken on the task of learning how Robert wanted to be treated. The time would come when I would show him my world and my definition of love, but right then it was about him. Instead of teaching one another how to respect ourselves, I was blindsided by my own insecurities. I had not taught myself how to treat myself yet.

Blame it on society, television, music, or the media, but from a young age girls are taught that a hero is coming to save them. Prince Charming has his choice of any woman in the land, and if he picks you, you're the luckiest girl in the world. We learn that we may have to become someone we aren't in order to win a man. At some point the clock will strike twelve; he'll see our flaws but still love us. Underneath all the quick banter and coy smiles, there's this little girl who's dying to be loved.

We take the holes from our abandonment issues, hearts torn by neglect, and staggered tears of broken promises and dress them up in a ball gown and glass slippers. Ticktock . . . ticktock. . . . The clock strikes twelve and we are completely bare, fully exposing ourselves to a man we pretended to be a princess to attract, only to be met with the bitter truth that we never really had it all together.

We just wanted to be better for him. We wanted to stand out in the crowd. Then life forced us to reveal our harsh truth: We were never strong enough to play this game. How can we ever desire a healthy whole relationship when we begin by accepting things we know hurt us? I made the mistake of thinking I was strong enough to withstand the ticking of the clock.

And I'm not the only one.

Every situation is not the same, but I've encountered a version of this story, like the familiar fairy tale it's based on, time and time again. Either we do all we can to keep him, or try to make him feel like we don't need him.

My friends tried to coach my heart on how to win this game. If you want to get someone, make him feel as insecure as you feel.

You can't increase

the level of infection

and still expect a cure

to the disease.

Beat him at his own game. Wait to text him back, don't pick up on the first ring, and definitely don't go running whenever he calls. He has a friend so you get a friend. Tell him you're going on a date, go a few days without talking, make him think that you're tough and hard to get. The more I tried to be like him, the more I felt like I was losing him.

It's incredible how we weigh our options. You can't increase the level of infection and still expect a cure to the disease. We play by the rules of the love game, then cry when we lose.

I decided, as dangerous as it may be, to wear my rags to the ball. I knew he would still come dressed as Prince Charming, but I wanted to be the one he showed his rags to someday. In my heart, I felt that my love and acceptance of his rags would make him see that you can still be a prince even if the world doesn't see your crown. I loved him the way I wanted to be loved, even though I knew he couldn't give it back to me fully.

He hardly gave any of himself away, so I would treasure whatever he did give me. In time he would see that he could give all of himself to me.

He and his ex (and how many others?) would be friends, and I would pretend to be the completely confident girlfriend. I bit my tongue when I saw them interact on Facebook. When I saw them sitting together in the cafeteria, I grabbed my lunch and sat with them. I couldn't let them know that they were getting to me. Each time I accepted something that bruised me but didn't break me, I lost.

The temperature began to drop, making for perfect weather as the TCU football season began winding down. I was glad. Robert and I were completely different when the roar of the crowd didn't drown my voice or blur his vision. Robert and his new friend had cooled down. Growing tired of my bottomless pit of "I don't care" shenanigans, she was moving on with her life.

I heard rumors on campus that she had someone new in her life. I wished them the best, too. I hoped that they went on to fall deeply in love, get engaged, have children, and move far away. As long as she left us alone, I didn't care how it happened. She no longer waited at the end of games; she hardly even came to the games at all.

Finally, it would just be the two of us again. Or so I thought.

One Friday before heading into practice, Robert called and asked if I would pick up his mother and sister from the bus station for the next day's game. I tried to act as casually as he was when he asked me, but I could hear the trumpets blowing. This was the next level and I wouldn't mess it up. Of course I would pick them up! I'd make sure they were settled in, fed, and comfortable while they were with me. And then he dropped a bomb before ending the call.

She knew about my emptying out her son's apartment, and she wasn't happy about it.

Unsure of how I would handle the meeting now, I called Stacia. She always helped me figure out the best thing to do. Stacia says the things I think but would never say. I say the things she feels but would never reveal. We've always been one another's ally. I don't get angry often; it takes too much out of me. It's not always healthy to just let things weigh on you either, though. With Stacia, I could be angry. I didn't understand what Robert told his mother, but I was almost sure it wasn't the full story.

I was stuck now. If I backed out, I would look like a coward. The way forward meant facing mama's wrath. But he was giving me a chance to see a side of his world that not many had been privy to. I could do this. So when I asked Stacia how I should handle the conversation if it came up, she told me to tell the truth.

The reason Stacia and I are always able to laugh even in intense situations is because of how differently we communicate. I like to tell gentle truths, while Stacia likes to tell it like it is. So my plan was to approach the situation with Robert's mom gently, and then if things escalated, I would bring out the Stacia in me.

Saturday morning, time sped by while I waited to make my way to downtown Fort Worth. I left early just to make sure I would be on time and wouldn't risk traffic. I had never seen Robert's mother before, but I was hoping that I would recognize her and his sister by his description. The moment the crowd dissipated I saw them. Had they all three been together they would have looked like triplets. I waved, purposely trying to not look either giddy or under enthused. As we approached each other, his mother forced a polite smile.

"You're much prettier than the ex-fiancée," she said, looking me up and down.

I was shocked, but Robert had warned me that they don't hold much back. I nodded and forced my own polite smile in return. This car ride would be interesting.

Once we got their bags and settled into the car, I took them to Robert's apartment. During the drive we chatted about safe topics, mostly about Robert, and warmed up to each other. But sweat starting beading on my nose when I put the key into the doorknob. His apartment had never really returned to its original glory after Operation Payback. His mother, Ms. Samantha, hadn't brought it up thus far, but I feared walking in would strike up the inevitable conversation.

"Mm-hmm," she said, looking around and then looking at me. "Now, what happened?"

"Well," I said and swallowed hard, stalling for another two seconds before deciding to tell her the truth. "I spent a lot of my savings, time, and energy into decorating a home for Robert, not a love nest for him and his ex-girlfriend."

She shook her head and then gave me a genuinely warm, knowing smile. "Well, a woman's got to do what a woman's got to do!"

I knew I was going to like this lady. And I couldn't wait to call Stacia.

As silly as it may seem, when people know who my father is, they tend to change who they are around me. Usually people try to be very righteous or holier than thou, thinking that this must be how we live our lives. But some go out of their way to prove that they don't care one way or the other. Robert and his family were so beautifully themselves, naturally sidestepping these extremes, that it intrigued me. They didn't filter their words or thoughts to make sure they were T.D. Jakes approved. Nor did they try to shock me by blatantly disparaging the church or his ministry.

Meeting them made me fall even more in love with Robert.

I always felt like I needed either to act a certain way to be in the church or to disown my religious roots to fit into the world. Either way I would have to change, but here they were, freely being themselves. Things weren't always said the most eloquently or even politely, but they said it. I loved how beautifully his mother and sister owned their truth. Once we got the apartment talk out of the way, the rest of the day was smooth sailing.

That same weekend, I learned that Robert had a son.

When we first met, Robert had told me about his daughter and about her sister, who wasn't biologically his but whom he cared for like his own. He had never mentioned a son—and clearly still didn't intend to. I guess I wasn't the only one afraid to give myself away.

Now that I knew, I desperately wanted to know more. Should I wait and let him feel comfortable enough to tell me the truth in his own time, or should I confront his omission?

Growing up in ministry, I had learned that people share when they're ready, not when they're forced. One day, after Robert told me the truth, I would tell him that I knew all along, but that I wanted him to tell me in his own time. He would see that I could be gentle with his shame, insecurity, or fears. I would prove to him that love could conquer all.

I knew I had my work cut out for me, that Robert was waiting for me to abandon him. When we first started spending hour after hour chatting, he shared a lot about his childhood with me. His younger brother had died in a house fire when he was young. In the middle of the night, Robert was awakened by smoke. After he helped get his mother and sister out of the fire, he wasn't able to go back in and get his brother.

I fell in love with the parts of him that I wanted to change about myself.

He carried the guilt with him for many years. He told me that coping was hard for their entire family. While some people turned to drugs, he turned to football. He wore that jersey for his brother, Rudy, and for himself. If he couldn't save him, he at least wanted to make him proud.

When I learned that Robert had a son, I wanted to run. It wasn't just that he had a son, but that he had hidden him, and so many other unknowns, from me. Robert was clearly afraid of the power of the truth, and so was I.

I fell in love with the parts of him that I wanted to change about myself. Misery loves company, and there was something appealing about knowing that I wasn't messed up on my own. The more I focused on his dysfunction, the less time I had to worry about my own. He became an incredible distraction from my own struggles. The more I worked on him, the less time I had to focus on what was wrong with me.

But by the end of the semester, my own weaknesses were staring back at me. School was one of the many things lost in competition with Robert. Of the five classes I was enrolled in, I would be lucky to pass two or three of them. Not excel. Not master. Barely grasp. Just pass by the skin of my teeth.

My parents were bound to find out. There was no way I could explain my failure without serious fallout. I prayed they would not force me to choose between school—which represented my blueprint for the future and my path of redemption—and Robert, who represented the only thing I could see in the present.

I was headed for a showdown.

7

Stripped

WHEN I RECEIVED my transcript at the end of the fall 2006 semester, I knew I was in serious trouble. As feared, I had passed only two of the five classes for which I originally enrolled. And those two grades were nothing to write home about, either. My parents surely knew something was going on with me. They had already reminded me earlier in the semester that they held me accountable for their investment in my college education. The message was clear: If I couldn't get it together on their dime, the next time I attended college it would be on my own.

So sitting down with them to reveal my grades, I was more than nervous.

I admitted to my distraction and attributed it to being caught up in the freedom that college brings. I made it less about my relationship with Robert and more about the overall transition. I didn't want to admit that I had become so distracted that I wasn't even sure I could finish college. They wouldn't want to hear that my time with

Robert was causing me to really question what I wanted. After taking and failing the prerequisite math course for my accounting degree, I started taking journalism courses.

Of all of my courses, the ones where I showed the most promise were always language associated. Anything that involved the passionate use of words intrigued me. My motivation for wanting the accounting degree remained with me: I wanted to recover from my pregnancy, and I felt the only way to do that was by helping my father. My pregnancy no longer made me a fit for ministry, so I was depending on an accounting degree to complete my recovery. As the semester came to a close, however, I knew that it would be impossible for me to successfully achieve that goal.

Our idea of forgiveness is often based on the idea that there must be recovery. We hardly ever isolate the two concepts.

I didn't have the strength to disappoint them again, though. For me, it was hard to believe that they were not supporting a future accountant. I couldn't grasp that they were just supporting *me*. Our idea of forgiveness is often based on the idea that there must be recovery. We hardly ever isolate the two concepts.

Seeking forgiveness doesn't mean that you have figured out the best way to recover. All it means is that you're committed to fixing what's been broken. As children we are taught that there is a punishment you pay in order for redemption to be granted. After being grounded, spanked, or having a toy taken away, we learn our lesson and life goes back to the way it was.

It's an awful trick we play on our youth. Because when we grow older, we learn that some decisions inherently follow you the rest of your life. No atonement can restore the way life used to be. The incarcerated serve their time and are released to a society that will constantly remind them that their past cast a shadow larger than their present.

Just because we've been forgiven doesn't mean we're free.

It then becomes our responsibility to use that shadow to hide our truth or protect others. Now, because of the shadow cast by my past, I hope others can be saved from the scorching pain of taking the same path I chose.

Will we use our shadow to take the heat off of others or to dim our own flame?

The more the misdirection of my past began to complicate my future, the more frustrated I became. What was the point in going to school if it wasn't for accounting? I had spent months selling the idea of becoming chief financial officer of The Potter's House. When I first shared my dream of becoming a CFO, I remember my father beaming with pride. I went on to explain how much job security the field offers.

My first real accounting assignment came when I had to add up how I had spent so much time away from home but had only two passing grades to show for it. My calculator failed me. There was no excuse.

How could I explain that I had spent that time making sure that Robert's paper was done and his apartment clean, while my heart was on life support? I spent Christmas break pleading my case with them, using freedom, transition, and (im)maturity all as excuses for my failure. Now that I had a chance to fully adjust, I could give my studies the attention they required.

For reasons I didn't understand then, but fully comprehend now, my parents gave me another chance. You see, my parents never expected that I wouldn't mess up again; they just wanted me to know and believe that better was possible for me. They were supporting me, not the dream I advertised for their benefit.

When we grow accustomed to being used, we anticipate that everyone wants something from us. But my parents never made us feel like we had to take on the weight of their calling. I carried that weight because it was what I thought I was supposed to do. Time after time, we fail at fitting into a perfect little box. Our childhood issues, mistakes, and fears don't make the prettiest corners.

Instead, we take the sharp edges of our lives and try to fit in and pray that our secret is never exposed. No, my biggest fear wasn't hurting myself or even others, and it wasn't because I was brave. I just didn't want anyone else to see exactly how much I didn't fit, especially my parents.

How could I admit that I was drowning when I was so busy gasping for air?

Instead of trusting my broken pieces with those who could cover me while I healed, I gave them to someone who could understand what it was like to be broken. Then cried when he broke them more. The vicious cycle of disappointment became comfortable for me. There was no chance for me to disappoint Robert because he was too busy disappointing me.

But maybe if I gave him what I needed, somehow he would find a way to give it back to me. I didn't want to change him; I just wanted to inspire him. I wanted to be enough for him to become better. I made him me. Supported him to my own demise, all to see if it was possible for love to truly conquer all.

I ignored those who were capable of throwing me a life jacket because I didn't want them to take a break and save me again. So when my parents gave me another chance, I didn't think they knew I was in trouble.

At the time my son was a toddler, but now that he is entering his tweenage years, I realize that there's no way your child drowns and water doesn't fill your own lungs. My parents were trying to save me. Somewhere in the ocean of my mess, they were on the coast offering me a way out, a chance to admit that I was lost.

Working with youth and speaking with parents at our church, I know there comes a point with your child, if you're anything like me, that you wonder where you went wrong. You question every decision you make. Did you do enough? Did you say it right? Was it too soon to move them? Too early to leave them?

There's no way your child drowns and water doesn't fill your own lungs.

I imagine you replay every decision that you think caused them to turn into someone you hardly recognize. Although I haven't gone through that stage as a parent yet, I can tell you from the other side that I knew I was drowning. There wasn't one day that passed where I didn't think that I was in too deep. The first and last thought of every evening was how I could get out. I wanted God to save me from myself, but I wasn't done thinking I could fix it myself.

We shun those who make us face ourselves because we aren't ready to see just how broken we are. My parents, each of them, would take off their clergy adornments, get into the water, and stand by me. They never forced me out or made me think that I had to choose. When they suspected I was drowning, but was too arrogant to ask for help, they stood beside me extending a lifeline.

I wasn't able to tell them I was in trouble, but at least I knew I wasn't alone.

There are formative years in our lives when we learn the harsh realities of life. No matter how much, as a parent, you'd like to protect your child, there are some lessons only life can teach.

You did what you could. Even if it wasn't the best, it was what you gave, and now you can choose to wash your hands of their mess or you can stand with them. Standing doesn't mean you agree, it doesn't mean you think they're right, and it certainly doesn't mean that it was what you dreamed for them. Standing only means that you're willing to partner with them and find a way out. Waiting and hoping for the moment when they finally place their hand in yours can be daunting.

It is the ultimate test of faith: giving your child back to Him.

When your child starts making the decisions that time-out can't cure, remember that you're merely a foster parent. Care, nurture, and help them until their Father makes His purpose clear in their lives. It won't be easy, but if Mary watched her child be crucified for God's glory, certainly we can trust that He will protect those who come to Him.

You may be the only gateway to God that they remember. Keep your heart pure and your faith strong.

After many conversations, the decision was made. I would move onto campus, where I'd be trusted to continue my studies without distraction, only coming home on the weekends to spend time with Chi. My parents would help me balance parenting while I made a better future for the both of us.

Three weeks into the spring semester of 2007, I completely stopped going to class.

I was no longer passionate about pursuing accounting, and the math course I had already failed twice was off to a less-than-stellar start. I didn't want to go home, I was too afraid. I didn't tell anyone except Robert. But I had a plan. If I got a job now, I could start saving enough money to get Chi at the end of the semester. That way I would still use the time to make a better life for us.

When I told Robert my plan, he asked if I was sure, but he didn't make it a big deal. Where he was from, the fact that he went to a university made him a hero. But he didn't care that I had lost any chance of receiving my own cape.

I called a friend of mine whose boyfriend played on the football team, too. Although she didn't go to school at TCU, she was always on campus and we had become friends. I told her I was looking for work and that I needed some pretty significant money. While I waited to hear from her, I continued looking for work on my own.

With no job experience and only some college to speak of, pickings were slim. Going out for interviews, I usually found myself in a reception area surrounded by people quite a bit more qualified than I was. The jobs I did get callbacks on were for commission-based jobs—selling knives, magazines, or some other product from door to door. I needed something that would be more reliable.

A friend called me and told me that she knew of a place that was hiring and that I could start the next day. I pulled up at the address and found a strip club. I called my friend, freaking out! Was she crazy? There was no way in the world I could strip. After saying a few words, not worth repeating here, she finally told me that I would be waitressing. It was easy, the tips were great, and I wouldn't have to actually be the entertainment.

The moment I stepped into the strip club, I saw a familiar face and left before they could see me. So this would be interesting. I called my friend and told her what happened. After we hung up, she sent me a picture of her tips for the evening: $300.

I could find another club. I told only one person besides Robert about my new career path—my best friend Stacia, who was now a law student. She didn't judge me, though. She knew that I was just doing what I had to do. She knew neither of us had been raised to live the way we were, but if we had to be lost, at least we were together.

I searched the outskirts of the metroplex for places that would be least likely to have someone who recognized my Jakes face. Almost everywhere I went, the waitresses were scantily clad or they were only hiring dancers. Having received no callbacks from my more traditional interviews and running out of luck on the fast money, I got discouraged.

When Robert got back to his apartment from practice one evening, I was sitting in the middle of the floor with my laptop, newspapers, and a pen. I had applied to at least twenty jobs a day. I told Robert that I would have to file to officially withdraw from school. If I couldn't find a job, the least I could do was make sure my parents got their money back.

Withdrawing meant moving home with no job and no plan. Before my imagination could begin to run wild, Robert offered to let me stay at his apartment. Of course, we'd be struggling. His check barely covered his expenses, but we could make it work. The next day I withdrew from school, then moved out of my dorm and into Robert's apartment.

Yes, I was shacking.

There comes a time in our lives when we combat with all of our might not to become the worst version of ourselves. We ingrain the image into our brain so that we can never forget who we could become. For some, it's the stepfather who abused your mother. For others, the mother who blocked you out with the wall she built around her heart. For me, it was failing. I would do anything to avoid disappointment on my parents' faces. I'd already done my fair share

If only we spent more

time embracing who

we are and less time

grieving who we thought

we were supposed to be.

of damage as it was. I'd rather try to make it on my own than have to admit I'd messed up again.

So I arrogantly masqueraded my fear as pride. I was an adult. I could make my own decisions. I spent the first couple of years with my son striving to outrun statistics. I excelled in high school because I wanted to repair the damage on my life's résumé. I wanted to prove that a pregnancy wouldn't define me for the rest of my life. I spent so much time running from my truth.

If only we spent more time embracing who we are and less time grieving who we thought we were supposed to be. I thought my greatest sin would be that I wasn't able to honor my son's life with a traditional upbringing. Turns out my relentless pursuit of correcting those wrongs left me more damaged than the pregnancy itself. I think God allows some things to happen so we are forced to seek Him. Foolishly, we pursue materialistic things knowing that it's not just because we need them for the pretty picture. We need the materials to cover the shame.

Broken, lost, hurt, and confused, I had no more material to cover up the shame of my worst fear being realized. I wouldn't be able to fix the mess I'd made in Malachi's life. I wouldn't be able to repair the damage the ministry took. I was flunking out of class for someone that made me feel like I was worth looking at. I think it's what made me fall in love with Robert.

If I could get Robert to love me, then maybe I wasn't damaged goods after all. All I had to do was get him to accept me. Then maybe I could be redeemed. He was the only thing I had left that wasn't a reminder of my failures. I genuinely loved him for that. Life is so hard when you fall in love with being numb. I didn't want to see my parents' irritation about my life, so I moved in with Robert. Needless to say, they were not pleased. When their disapproval turned to flat-out disappointment, I stopped calling.

It's hard to explain why I chose Robert, especially given our history and where I stand now. In many ways we were both trying to outrun the statistics of our past. I believed that if I loved him to health, then maybe he could figure out how to heal me in return. Our love was genuine, but it wasn't healthy. Love does conquer all, but it must be used in its purest form. Love is too often diluted with lust, money, pain, and abuse.

I didn't know that then, of course. All that mattered to me was that I had love, or what passed for it. Teen moms don't get fairy tales, but I was determined to make my relationship with Robert the exception. We would prove wrong everyone who doubted us. I just had a few unexpected detours on the way.

Love does conquer all, but it must be used in its purest form. Love is too often diluted with lust, money, pain, and abuse.

While out one day job hunting, I ended up on a side of town I had never been before. There wasn't a familiar exit for miles and miles. It looked like the Texas I imagined in West Virginia. Then, there it was. Off in the distance, standing higher than anything else around it, Texas Cabaret.

I pulled up to the building, parked my car, took a deep breath, and then went in. The topless club was pretty crowded. I noted that the waitresses wore a black top with black pants. There were three dancers on the stage. Before I could see anything else, the bouncer asked if he could help me with anything.

I was hired on the spot. No questions, no trial period. I trained that day and started the next.

There are these moments in life when we imagine who we want to become. Before the vision is fully realized in our mind, we are awakened by the harsh reality of who we are and what we have done. The distance between point A and point B stretches further than our faith allows and we give in. We cave in to the reality of our existence and give the ladder of hope to someone who has what it takes to go the distance.

Sure, waitressing at a strip club wasn't the ideal job for the daughter of Bishop and Mrs. Jakes, but I had to survive. It took too much work, hope, and energy to attempt to live my dream. My co-workers at the club had no idea who they were working with; that didn't bother them or me.

Life doesn't take a break on anyone. All of us, sooner or later, will face incredible blows. Maybe they're meant to strengthen us, but when you're on the receiving end, it feels like it was meant to break us. Instead of rising to the occasion and squaring back off, we give in to the disappointment.

We gravitate to people who are too busy tending to their own mess that they have no time or energy to focus on our own. I found myself in the safety of ignorance. They didn't know who I was, who I could have become, or why I had ended up there. All that mattered when I entered the dark building was that I had enough cash in my pocket to make change.

Each day I walked into the club, I felt shame. I let the shame comfort me because it was easier than love challenging me. In this space it was okay to be broken; it was okay to not want more.

I was lost and wasn't sure if I could even be found anymore.

I worked at the club for over a month. I'd make small talk with the waitresses, but nothing too in-depth. They were friendly enough and I was quiet enough that we hardly had any issues.

I did not want that to be my life, but I didn't see how anything else was possible. I gave up on me. On the sidelines of my life there were many people cheering me on. The cheers that were meant to motivate me scared me. I didn't want to disappoint them by telling my secret: I was playing a game and didn't know the rules. Little did I know that this wasn't just my secret.

For years, everyone familiar with my last name expected that life was somehow much easier for us. With wide eyes and hopeful voices they asked, "What's it like to be in that family?" I wanted to give them some type of hope that somewhere on the other side of the mountain there's this place where you no longer have pain, secrets, or shame. I knew that, like me, they wanted to believe there was more to life than our current place.

I had no hope to sell anyone.

How could I tell them that you exchange one problem for another? None of us are born with a map. There's no clear-cut plan on how to avoid trouble. We face critical life moments with no preparation and then become penalized for getting the answer wrong. I didn't just give up on myself, I gave up because I was tired of failing. I graduated at sixteen years old in the top percent of graduates in the nation. A member of the National Honors Society, I was selected to go to Washington, D.C., where I was commended with a group of my peers for my commitment to my education. You would've thought that I paid my teachers when you read my recommendation letters for college.

On the sidelines of my life there were many people cheering me on. The cheers that were meant to motivate me scared me.

Two years later, I was learning the difference between being among top-shelf peers and watching the young faces of other women like me settle into survivor mode. Dreams were for people who hadn't experienced failure; life was for the rest of us.

So why share this with you?

Whether you were born with a silver or plastic spoon in your mouth, it doesn't determine who you become. There has to be some fight in you. You have to be willing to become uncomfortable if you want to be stretched. There's no way we get from point A to point B without recognizing that there will be pain.

If we're lucky, we understand that the pain is growing us, but there will be days when all we can focus on is the hurt and the disappointment of being utterly broken. And, to be honest, sometimes it's easier to be surrounded by people who know and don't judge your brokenness than to come around those who want to infect you with their opinions.

Instantly, I knew what had happened to the people I grew up with who stopped coming to church. Little by little, our childhood entourage of ten to fifteen dwarfed to three or four. The others had learned, like I eventually did, that there was a whole group of people outside the walls of our church who would accept us broken and weren't interested in condemning us. We could be our imperfect selves out there, but in the church or in our homes there were questions for which we had no answers.

The answers don't come because you're a pastor and certainly not because you're a pastor's daughter. I had to find my way, just like you. My journey wasn't beautiful and it certainly wasn't clean. Your life doesn't have to resemble a fairy tale for your dream to come true. I wish I could tell you that I was born into a family that got to escape trouble just because God gifted my dad with an incredible gift of interpreting the Bible. The truth is that our gifts come at a cost.

We never grew up believing in Santa Claus, something for which we jokingly say we should probably seek counseling. After having my own children and Christmas to prepare for, I understood how disheartening it is to work all year for someone else to take credit for the gifts that you give your children. When we opened our presents, we knew that we got them because our parents worked tirelessly to give them to us. We knew what it cost them to make us smile.

Very few people know the cost of ministry. Anytime you give away something that's in you, you lose a piece of you. We trust that God will restore all that we have poured out for His glory. We pray that He's covering us while we share His Word, but it is still a test of faith to leave your own home unguarded while you help others to rebuild. My parents' gift didn't save me from trouble, but it did plant a seed inside of me.

In the darkness of a strip club, dirt covered the seed that was in my heart.

If we aren't careful, we will confuse the dirt that covers the seed of our destiny for a final burial. We have to be buried so that we can be rooted before emerging into the world. No one can grow your roots for you. But you get to decide whether your darkest moments become the death of you or the roots in you. I was applying for jobs during the day and working at the club at night. I didn't want to be in accounting, but I couldn't be a waitress forever. I wanted my son and I couldn't work the late nights. Something had to come through job-wise before the semester ended, otherwise I would be devastated.

One day while I was heading to work, my uncle called and asked if we could meet. I told him I was on my way to work. As far as my family knew, I was working at an actual restaurant by campus.

When he offered to come in, and we could talk while I worked, I knew something was going on.

I called in to the club and told them I was sick.

At least that was true.

An hour later, I was in tears with my uncle Sean. My mother knew that something was going on with me, but because I wasn't talking, she and my uncle conspired to find out how much trouble I was in. They knew I wasn't in school, living in my dorm, or working at a restaurant. My uncle, also in charge of security at the church, made a few phone calls and found out exactly where I was working. Having never gone in to see exactly what I was doing at the Texas Cabaret, they assumed I was stripping.

I wasn't upset. How could I be?

We're all one heartbreak away from bitterness, one bad decision away from calamity.

I understood too well that life doesn't always go as planned. It was pretty unlikely that the girls dancing on the poles were there because they had dreamed of it since they were little girls. Life for them, like me, had led them to make some decisions that were in direct contrast to the fairy tales we grew up watching. There wasn't much difference between us. We're all one heartbreak away from bitterness, one bad decision away from calamity.

I was afraid of disappointing my family with my truth. I didn't want them to see how low I was. I tried to play hide-and-seek, but love found me. My mother had given my uncle one charge: "When you find my baby, bring her back to me." On the car ride home, thousands of things crossed my mind. I wondered whether I was walking into an intervention, confrontation, or prison. I wasn't sure how my parents were going to react. When I knocked on the door of my parents' bedroom, my mother answered the door and I fell into her arms. There was no need for words. I just needed to feel her arms around me. I needed to remember what it felt like to be held together.

That was my last day working at the strip club.

I was shattered, but there in her arms I felt like I was whole again. There comes this opportunity in all of our lives when we must choose between becoming completely enraged and being silent. Determining which reaction is best is never easy. Just remember when you're dealing with a person who is weary, you don't want your rage to add to their brokenness. You see, most of the time, you don't need someone to tell you you're wrong. You carry the grief of being lost with every turn you make. The last thing you need when you're stranded is someone yelling at you to find your way.

> *The last thing you need when you're stranded is someone yelling at you to find your way.*

There's no worse feeling than being lost in a strange land. I could get lost in the church and it never scared me, because I knew that I would eventually find my way or someone would find me. When I dropped out of school and started applying for jobs, I was in unchartered territory. I learned to make a résumé online. No one called in any favors to find me a job. I had spent most of my life wanting someone to see only *Sarah* Jakes, not Sarah *Jakes*. I wanted someone to care that I was someone other than T.D. Jakes's daughter.

The one thing I had spent years seeking had been there all along. In my mother's arms, I realized that my parents were the ones who cared about Sarah. They were the ones who didn't need to use me to further their own agendas. I was their daughter. Right, wrong, broken, or afraid, I was still theirs.

The best way to teach others, especially your children, about God is loving them. Before our babies can say *Bible*—let alone read it, understand it, and apply it to their lives—they know love. They understand that someone has been taking care of them when they couldn't take care of themselves. They learn that love sometimes means sacrifice. We must work so that they can play, cook so that they can eat, and run so that they can eventually fly.

We don't teach our children to speak; they listen and learn based on what we say. They watch the form our mouth makes when we prepare for words to come out. They study when to use which phrase appropriately. We teach love the same way.

How can we expect adults to understand that love is about being there when love for them meant being left alone to find their own way? How do we teach that love is about sacrifice when all we do is take? We can't expect others to understand our selfless love when all they've known is looking out for themselves.

When I left my parents' home, I made two decisions: I was quitting my job and Robert was going to learn my definition of love.

Both would cost me.

8

Wedding Bells

WE WERE BROKE.

Not just living check to check, but getting eviction notices, waiting for the electricity to be turned off, and sharing a cup of noodles for dinner. It had been a week since the day at my parents' when I decided to quit working at the club. We paid as many bills as we could given my unexpected moral epiphany. And I was excited to have a job interview for a position that didn't require me to sell knives, cleaning supplies, magazines, or meat to get paid.

If I landed the job, I'd be working through a temp agency as a receptionist. It wasn't accounting or journalism, but it was a start. I would get paid weekly and have benefits. I managed to make it past the first round of interviews with the agency; the next round was with the actual company.

It was Valentine's Day, though, and there was no way on our budget to have reservations at a fine restaurant. I had taken a few odd jobs baby-sitting and cleaning homes, but it was nothing compared with the tips I had been receiving at the club. By the time we put gas in our cars, we couldn't even do a good grocery run. We survived on fast food, dollar store necessities, and ramen noodles.

But I was determined to stitch together some kind of special, romantic dinner. So I gathered up some of my old CDs, DVDs, and books and went to a resale store, hoping I could get enough to make us a nice dinner. I got a whole $30, but my gas tank was empty. I put $15 in the tank, then went to an ice cream shop and got our favorite combinations. After that I went to Dollar Tree and got frozen fries. Our cozy, candlelit dinner was ice cream and fries. It was the best I could do.

Juggling my purchases, I opened the door of the apartment and my mouth flew open. Robert had laid a blanket down on the living room floor, got our favorites from all the local fast food restaurants, and lit candles.

Who needed a fancy restaurant—or ice cream and fries, for that matter—when we had each other?

***

When you meet someone you suspect can do more to hurt you than enhance you, you grab every strand of hope extended. Regardless of our past, I clung desperately to every kind word and sweet gesture Robert offered. Any time he showed a small sign of becoming the kind of person I dreamed of, it was easier to stay a little longer. It wasn't a balanced scale, but the hope he gave me was enough for me to stay.

I told myself he was on his way and that it would be worth the wait. I told myself that the more I loved him the right way, now with my family behind me (were they?), I could show him how incredible we could be. I had to help him see himself the way I did when he was at his best.

Regardless of how positive we try to be, there's this quiet voice in our head that recognizes the statistics aren't easily dismissed. Part of growing up means realizing that relationships are hard work, not sweet chick flicks or fairy-tale romances. We hear the songs about heartbreak and see the relationships around us that have fallen apart, and we'd rather accept an imperfect love than no love at all.

We tell our loneliness that it won't last long, but it doesn't hear us because we are with someone and still feel alone. Some company is better than none. When we accept that we are no longer worth more than what we have, we accept that others don't see us that way either. We try to convince them that we're worth it while their actions just remind us that we aren't.

Having the foresight to look beyond surviving the moment and seeing a prosperous future is dreaming. Making a plan to get there is ambition.

Ultimately, in most relationships I think that we confuse love and respect. The two are not mutually exclusive, but I had no way of knowing that because I had never known love that didn't come with respect. My parents' marriage modeled integrity, honesty, sacrifice, and leadership. They had a plan and a promise that they made to each other, and to us, and they kept it.

Having the foresight to look beyond surviving the moment and seeing a prosperous future is dreaming. Making a plan to get there is ambition. That same ambition was inside of me, misdirected at times, but in me nonetheless. I had a plan and a vision and I would see it through. I might get scarred and bruised along the way, but it was possible for me to win.

If I could just survive long enough.

"You look great, baby," my mom said. She had called me to see if we could have lunch before my interview. We were relearning one another, and I wanted her to know that she wasn't going to lose me again.

"Thanks, Mom," I said, hugging her and remembering how safe I felt in her arms only the week before. "I'm nervous about the job."

"Just be yourself," she said confidently. "Everything else okay?" She raised an eyebrow in the way that mothers have to let you know what the unspoken question really is.

"Yes, ma'am," I said, trying to convince us both. We proceeded to enjoy lunch and catch up about other members of our family. Being with her made me feel calm and relaxed, like it all truly was going to be okay.

When we hugged good-bye, it was one of those holding-me-together hugs. She forced two hundred-dollar bills into my hand and told me to take care of myself. I started to protest, but I needed the money.

After such encouragement on every level from my mother, I went to my interview determined to get the job. I was surprised when I pulled up to Meacham Airport, a small municipal airport in Fort Worth. I had assumed that I would be interviewing in an office building, not at an airport.

Turns out the company that was looking for a receptionist was a contractor for the air force. With the supervision of in-house military support, the company prides itself on being the "leading supplier of aerospace and defense products to the U.S. government, its allies, and major prime contractors." After some small talk and questions about my work history, the interview was over. I wasn't sure how to gauge whether it went well or not; the interviewers were pleasant but a little hard to read. They did tell me that I would know something either way by the week's end.

Noticing the time, I knew traffic would be congested on the high-ways leading back to my home, so I plugged my address into my phone and started taking back roads. Within five minutes I was passing Texas Cabaret, my previous employer. Had I ever served any of the people I was hoping to work for? The place was pretty popular for lunch specials and entertainment. How mortifying would it be to walk in the first day of a new job and report to someone I'd seen drunk and hitting on strippers just weeks before! Or worse, what if they recognized me?

My phone rang and it was the temp agency. I sent the call to voice mail, not wanting to pull over for a conversation in which I'd have to fake understanding if I didn't get the job. Using the money my mom had given me, I stopped to get some groceries and a little pick-me-up treat for myself. In the middle of cooking dinner, I remembered to check the voice mail from the agency.

I got the job!

All I needed was one shot and I had it. I would prove myself invaluable to the company and hopefully work my way up. I was ready to have some security. Robert and I celebrated with ice cream and fries. When I called my mom, she offered to get me some work clothes, since I was officially a career woman.

> *Maybe we aren't as lost as we think we are. We just can't see beyond the shame of being lost in the first place.*

I was struck by how things were finally turning around. It seemed like the moment I admitted that I was lost, I was one step closer to being found. How poetic that the club was within just a few minutes of the airport where I had been hired.

Maybe we aren't as lost as we think we are. We just can't see beyond the shame of being lost in the first place. One of the goals of Christians is to learn to see ourselves the way our Creator sees us. The problem is that most of us can't get over how we see ourselves. Our reality is so obviously flawed that the idea that someone, let alone God, is willing to look past that is incomprehensible. We forget that He sees the full picture, even when we fail, too.

So while objects in the mirror "may appear closer than they are," as the song goes, we forget that this only applies because the mirror is curved. When we have been bent and turned by life, our perspective begins to change and our future becomes distorted.

Perhaps my reconciliation with my parents and a new, more respectable career choice would help undo some of the bends that life had created. I was beginning to see my way out. The reflection of my future seemed a little clearer.

Looking back on that moment, I see that I was still focusing on the closeness of my pain. God wanted me to see that I was looking at the wrong mirror. His image of me had all my flaws, distortions, and mistakes, but it also held my purpose, hope, and joy. Perhaps our biggest issue is not that we can't see ourselves; it's that we can't accept that even when we're broken, His love for us has not been distorted.

With my past just behind me, I tried to focus on how I could maximize the opportunity in my present. At work I stopped wondering whether anyone would recognize me and began to learn the company.

Perhaps our biggest issue

is not that we can't see

ourselves; it's that we can't

accept that even when we're

broken, His love for us has

not been distorted.

Within a few weeks I was doing the payroll for over a hundred subcontractors and completely organizing the office break areas and supply rooms. Anytime I received a task, I turned it around as quickly as possible. I worked ten hours a week more than my temp contract required so that I could help when large projects were due, hoping that if I showed enough initiative they would make me a full-time employee. Which would mean even more security for us.

Whenever the contractor made a proposal to the government, we had to create large binders with time frames, project schedules, budget needs, and expected outcomes. I started off helping a program manager with the filing, but as I proved my accuracy, I was trusted to do them on my own, happy to alleviate some of the burden of the program managers, who didn't have any support staff.

Besides learning the ropes, I also made friends. I was hired during one of the busiest times for them, but when things slowed down I started going to lunch with a few members of the staff. I got to learn about the other people in the building. They taught me who was friendly and who was not so friendly.

One of my friends, Stefanie, had been the receptionist for seven years before me. She knew who would or would not speak when coming in, how many calls they received on average, and how they liked their coffee. With her guidance, I learned what the remaining staff expected from me. I wanted to have the type of longevity that she had, so I soaked in every word.

On slow days I would wander upstairs to Terrie's office. She worked with contracts and often allowed me to help her create the proposals. While we sifted through paper work, we shared bits and pieces of our stories with one another. I started calling her my second mom. She was constantly looking out for me and giving me advice on how to make myself an asset to the company.

Since a lot of the contractors could be a little aggressive toward women, she taught me how to communicate pleasantly without giving the wrong impression. She had her children at a younger age and understood what I was trying to do with my life. Her encouragement helped me settle into my new role there.

I'm convinced my position there was a test of my faith. I was in a field I knew nothing about. Daily, words would fly by my head that I couldn't define even with a dictionary. Government terms, the alphabet soup of acronyms, and information about specific weapons were daily topics. This little church girl had found herself in the real world, and I was determined to succeed.

Our biggest tests of faith don't always come in the ways we expect. When we've lost our way in life, we usually have nothing left but our faith to guide us. While challenging, these tests are neither blissful nor miserable but simply the quiet moments in our life when we question whether He is still with us. I saw my receptionist job as an opportunity to show God that even though I hadn't excelled the way I wanted to, I still had the desire to be great, even if it was just at answering phones.

So many people end up in roles they never wanted to play, but life left them with no other part. Instead of making the best of the situation, they punish all those they encounter with the bitterness from a dream deferred. Unable to let go of what could have been, they choose to make the present pay for the mistakes of their past. Seldom do they realize that while they grieve their dream, those around them grieve any hope of knowing their true identity.

Your life may not be where you want it to be, but things could be so much worse. If you don't learn to adjust to the shifts in your life, the shifts will change you. One day you'll wake up and you won't have a clue who you have become. You will remember the days when your smile reached your eyes and laughter cleansed your soul as distant, unreachable times.

The next time you find yourself at a rest stop on the road to destiny, look for the wildflowers blooming along the road's shoulder. The beauty may seem fragmented or not as neat and contained as you would like, but it's still there.

Even though your life may not be what you wanted, it's still a life that someone else isn't here to enjoy. It's *yours*. If we don't learn to utilize our hope to combat our disappointment, our hearts become tarnished. What once was so beautiful has been left to rust, all because we didn't take the time to remain present to the changes within us.

If there is anything more devastating than heartbreak, it has to be the feelings we carry when we feel we've lost our destiny. When the things we hoped for feel so incredibly out of reach, we resent our surroundings because it's not what we envisioned. Somehow during these times we must learn to thank God for His provision. I'm convinced how you handle a setback will determine the strength of your comeback.

Each day we wake up we must make a decision to become a better person. The next time you find yourself at a rest stop on the road to destiny, look for the wildflowers blooming along the road's shoulder. The beauty may seem fragmented or not as neat and contained as you would like, but it's still there.

I searched for the blooms at my new place of employment and I found them. I didn't have the background to be in the field or the experience to be in the position, but I had the job. I could've come in each day begrudging the fact that I wasn't on a campus, but I decided to survive and pick a few wildflowers along the way.

By April I found a quaint three-bedroom townhome not too far from my job. Well outside the city limits, the rent was low enough to fit our growing but still small budget. I started searching sites like Craigslist for furniture. I could furnish it piece by piece, but most important was making sure that Malachi had his room. My mother joined in my excitement about finally finding my footing.

When she heard that we were picking up a washer and dryer from an online posting, she offered to get us a new set as a housewarming gift. Until then I had been going to the Laundromat after work to wash our clothes. I was prepared to do the same thing until we could afford to buy a set ourselves, but I was so tired of lugging the laundry around town. Growing up we had nannies or housekeepers who did our laundry. Now I was in the real world, away from the safety of home trying to find my way.

I knew it wasn't easy for either of my parents to accept how drastically my life had changed, but they held on to me—even though many would have opted to shun their children for not meeting their expectations. Instead, my parents adjusted their expectations to fit my current mindset. Step by step, when I was ready to make another move in the right direction, they flanked me on either side.

Robert and I were going to church every Sunday, even though we were living in sin. We had so many problems to sort through, we tackled each one as we could. Things had gotten much better fidelity-wise, not to say there wasn't any suspicion. It seemed like home life had really settled us. I couldn't afford to indulge in the shenanigans I was in before. I had to keep my job, and I didn't want anyone to overhear that I was going to fight someone in the parking lot at one of our football games. My job made me more responsible and cognizant that I had something to lose.

I had gone so long without winning; I couldn't bear to go back to the desperate job search or wondering if we would have enough money for groceries next week. While Robert attended school, I supported our needs and even some wants. Still, the memories of the apartment haunted me. I would be so glad when we would finally be able to start fresh. I was still saving for furniture when we got the keys, so we decided that we would save as much as we could until Robert's lease was up at the apartment. Still, things were really looking up.

My mother called one Saturday and asked when she could drop off the washer and dryer at the new place. I told her I could meet her over there that day. I got there, unlocked the house, and waited. I heard the wheels of the truck pull up, my mother in her car trailing behind. I told the guys where the laundry connections were and rushed to show my mom the rest of my new home. When I finished showing her upstairs, I walked downstairs to the guys in the truck placing a black leather sofa in the living room. I glanced back up at my mom and then ran to the truck. There was a house full of furniture in there.

My mouth fell open. . . . I had no words. More than likely without my father's knowledge, my mother took a moment to polish my crown and remind me where I came from. I said very few words, but the tears never stopped. I forgot what it felt like to be loved just because, by someone expecting nothing in return.

And little by little, the bends that distorted my self-image were undone.

And while I know there is a mentality that would suggest you give up on your child until they start to resemble the person you raised, I believe that relationship with God helps us determine the difference between a rebellious child and a hurting one. There is wisdom in knowing not to wiggle when your head is in the lion's mouth.

My parents did not want to lose me, because no matter how much I tried to fit into the world, they could still see my value. I was their diamond. I was covered in soot, dirt, disappointment, and fear, but my mother wanted to remind me that it was still possible for me to find my sparkle. I knew that buying the furniture was more than her just helping me, it was her gently polishing her child.

I was a diamond, covered in soot, dirt, disappointment, and fear, but my mother wanted to remind me that it was still possible for me to find my sparkle.

Robert entered his junior year of playing at TCU. Like most players, he dreamed of making it to the NFL, but he was also excited about entering federal law enforcement if the opportunity to turn pro didn't come. But he remained convinced that if he worked hard enough, the pro scouts would take notice. He knew he probably wouldn't be an early-round pick, but just the chance to play for one of the NFL teams we all watched on Sunday afternoons would be a dream come true. Robert's coach and other players he knew encouraged him that he might really have a shot if he continued to work hard and didn't lose focus.

I was still working as a temp with the government contractor, but I was hoping to get on permanently soon. I decided to try to get an idea of whether they felt I was a good fit for the company by making them aware that I had been offered another position.

News spread quickly that I could be leaving soon. Many of the actual air force controllers had taken a liking to me. When they heard that I could possibly be leaving, they offered me a job as their office manager before I could get an answer from my current employer. I confided in Terrie about the new opening. I didn't want to appear disloyal, but the opportunity to work directly for the air force and to actually have a salary was tempting.

I was getting paid $12 an hour as a receptionist. When I received the letter offering a $37,500 salary, as a nineteen-year-old with little experience and only some college, I knew I had to take it. After a trip to Boston to the headquarters for the air force division employing me, I went back to Texas with the paper work required to receive my government clearance and military contractor ID badge.

Only months before, I had been serving drinks at a strip club down the road, and now I was beginning to discover talents I didn't even know I had. While I was still working to mend the insecurities of our past, Robert and I began discussing the idea of marriage. I didn't want to continue living outside of God's will, especially since He had been so merciful to me as I found my way. With so many things in my life changing for the better, surely Robert would, as well.

So when he popped the question and agreed to ask my parents for their blessing, I said yes. This was what I wanted, wasn't it?

We found a ring on Craigslist, and Robert used all of his $600 school check to cover the cost of it. There was no big fancy date with a formal proposal; he simply gave me the ring once the transaction was completed, and then we went to dinner to celebrate the next step of our journey. He reminded me that when we first met and started having problems with the other women, he had promised me one thing: "All roads lead back to you."

I wanted a small wedding, no more than seventy-five people in my parents' living room. However, the closer it got to our June 21, 2008, wedding day, the invitation list and extravagance of the wedding grew. After spending so many years fighting to have things my way, it was nice to see my parents excited about something that had to do with me again. It seemed like there might be light at the end of the tunnel for me after all. I was looking forward to having stability and proving that I was capable of turning my life around.

The week of the wedding, we had 350 confirmed guests with more surprise elements than they were willing to share with me. The excitement, stress, and drama hung in the air like clouds. Robert's two daughters would be in the wedding and were coming in with his mother.

Earlier, before our engagement, he had finally opened up to me about the son I already knew about. Robert explained that when he became a standout in high school, a few people started viewing him as a ticket out of their hometown. He wasn't sure if the child was his, although he did try to do the right thing for a while before leaving.

Even without the certainty that the child was his, I suggested that we ask him to be in the wedding or at minimum attend. I didn't want his child to feel like we were starting a family without him. The boy's mother declined, so I didn't push.

Still, our wedding plans rolled along.

Thursday before the wedding, our entire wedding party went to a comedy show. Robert and his friends were in one car, me and mine in another. On the way out of the packed parking lot, we followed one another so that we could stick together. One car in particular kept trying to cut me off, and when unsuccessful, its driver yelled obscenities at me. I ignored them since they would have to wait like everyone else.

Before I knew it, the car pulled up alongside us and someone threw a beer bottle at me before speeding off. I didn't even have a chance to process the event when I saw Robert jump out of his car and take off on foot in the direction of my assailant. In the distance I saw him beating on the trunk of her car. His sister, Tiffany, in the car with me, began yelling to be released to help her brother.

My sister, Cora, opened her door, and we watched Tiffany race off in her brother's direction. She flung the car door open and started hitting the inebriated driver repeatedly. A family friend, out with us for the evening, pulled the two of them away from the car as quickly as he could. The whole thing was over before it started, but not before real damage was done. As Robert walked back to me, I noticed that his arm was covered in blood. He had punched the girl's window out and had a five-inch cut in the crease of his elbow.

Robert wasn't shaken up nearly as much as I was. He showed no signs of being in pain. When we made it to the emergency room and the nurse asked him what happened, he simply told her, "I thought someone hurt my wife." The parking lot scuffle was a strange encounter but clearly demonstrated to me how strongly he felt about me. Robert truly was loving me the best way he knew how.

Two days later, I walked down the aisle. When my eyes finally caught his, I noticed a steady stream of tears. My eyes were dry, though, because I couldn't afford to break down. By that point I was too far gone. I knew that I wasn't marrying a perfect man, but

I also knew he loved me. We would both have to be strong enough to grow with each other.

I smiled for the pictures and enjoyed my wedding day, but inside I had placed a wall around my heart. What had I agreed to when I said "I do"?

9

The Honeymoon's Over

OUR HONEYMOON WAS beautiful. From the moment we got in the car and headed for the airport, Robert treated me like a queen. Maybe marriage had given him the extra push he needed to step up. My mind wandered with the possibilities of our love coming into full bloom. And I was still floating on cloud nine when we returned home to Dallas, refreshed and ready to build an indestructible marriage with my more dedicated partner.

The news of our wedding circulated on the Internet at lightning speed. Somehow our photographer's site was hacked and over three hundred of our private wedding photos were released. The comments ranged from genuine congratulations, questions about our age, speculation that I was pregnant, or either of us marrying the other for money. Some of the comments hurt, but for the most part I let it roll off my back.

Then I saw a comment on YouTube I couldn't ignore. Some woman was claiming that Robert had a son with her that he wasn't taking care of. Since we briefly discussed the questionable paternity of his son, I approached him about getting closure or being more involved.

"We can talk about it later," he said.

The woman's comment had already garnered some attention. People were replying, asking for more information, suggesting my father pay her to be quiet, and definitely checking her motives. Frustrated with the accusations, she continued to defend herself and her son. The more upset she became, the more information she revealed. I wanted to respect my husband's wishes and leave it alone, but I also wanted to know more. So I Googled the birth records for the county where he grew up to see exactly how many children he had. It took some work, but once I found it, the truth couldn't be denied.

Four.

Robert had four children. The story about the younger sister he simply cared for wasn't true; she was his as well. I already knew about his son, but no one had mentioned another child that carried his name. Listing their ages was like counting down 7, 6, 5, and 4. There were four children by three different women.

I called my mother, upset. We hadn't been married a full month, and we were already breaking down. This was trust? This was communication? Four?

My mother remained calm and did the best she could to strengthen her newlywed daughter. "Darling," she said, "you knew that choosing him would mean there would be work. All of the children have mothers. Your job is to support their parenting efforts, not to take over."

I sighed, knowing she had to pull from a deep place to give me that answer. As devastated as I was, I could only imagine what it was like to release your daughter to someone who didn't take full ownership of the four pieces of him that were a mere two hours away.

This lie, added to another secret that we held back from our family, thickened the wall that existed around my heart. How could he ever fully give me pure love if he was struggling to love and accept his own children?

We were married now, and there wasn't much I could do about it. Tens of thousands of people were waiting to hear we failed. I repeated my mother's advice in my head over and over until it sunk in enough for me to go home. There would be no point in fighting or arguing. It didn't change the fact that the children were his and I couldn't leave.

No matter how much you accept an insecure person, you can never make them love or accept themselves. I kept telling myself that if I showed Robert he was still lovable, he would no longer need the validation of other women. It was larger than just the women, though.

At the root of our problem was that I wanted so badly for us to heal, and it felt like all he wanted was a distraction from his pain. Any reminder of his brokenness was an attack. I learned before marriage that yelling at him to do better wasn't making our situation better. I learned to quietly suffer and pray constantly while I hoped the man I loved would learn to love himself.

We were only two months into our marriage when I asked the counselor at our church if she would be willing to talk to us. Dr. Nicole created a treatment plan to aid both of us in healing. She had only one rule, and that was full disclosure. So I told her the secret that had caused my heart to be surrounded by brick and mortar.

A month and a half before our wedding, Robert started a relationship with someone else. She was a fellow student at TCU, and I found out about their relationship when a $60 restaurant charge was debited from our account. The night in question he had come home with one box of food. He told me he'd stopped on the way home from practice to get his favorite pasta, so I grabbed the fork and we ate together.

Since the hard days of living in the apartment, I had become obsessive about our money. Afraid of being near destitute again, I check our accounts daily. So the next day when I saw the charge, I knew that more than one person had eaten. Afraid to bring it up to Robert because I knew he would find an excuse, I called an acquaintance to see if she knew or could find out who Robert was seeing.

Within minutes she told me that he was seeing a girl down the hall from her dorm. She'd seen them leave together the day before; the girl came back with food from the same restaurant. When I confronted Robert about her, he left the house instantly. I called him a thousand times and left text messages laced with obscenity after obscenity.

We were six weeks from being married. We were already receiving wedding gifts, and the printed invitations had just gone out. My dad had started working more the year before just to make sure I had a fairy-tale wedding to this man I had shunned my entire family to be with. And now he was having dinner dates with coeds from campus?

When Robert finally came home the next day, he told me that he was nervous about the wedding. She was just a friend, someone he could talk to and nothing more.

The girl had a different story. When I contacted her on Facebook, I asked her for her version of the events. She told me that Robert was no longer happy with me and that I could put the wedding dress away. She went on to tell me about the many times they spent together and the things they laughed at concerning me.

Robert called her claims ludicrous. They were friends and nothing more; she was just bitter because she wanted to be with him and he rejected her. I had heard this song before. I was stuck between the lies he told me and the lies he told her.

I called my old acquaintance to see if she had any insight she could offer me. She told me that she would see if the girl was willing to say any more. Within hours, I knew their entire history. She told me everything she knew, and I thanked her because I knew I should've never asked her to be in our mess.

I took my time before reacting. Robert had already told me his version of the truth, and bringing it up again would only make the situation worse. He'd called her every name in the book. He fortified his story by reminding me groupies were a part of being with a football player. I would have to learn to trust him or them.

Any time your right to feel, think, and communicate has been stifled, you're in trouble.

Any time your right to feel, think, and communicate has been stifled, you're in trouble. In my heart, I knew Robert loved me. Even during these moments, I told myself that he was lying to protect me. Why go to such extremes if he didn't care about my feelings? I continued to accept love on his level, even though it brought me down. I wasn't allowed to be insecure. I was supposed to be strong enough to not be bruised by these instances of people trying to tear us apart.

Somehow, I was supposed to ignore that he was the one who gave them the bullets to use against me. Had he never opened the door, she wouldn't be in our lives, I argued. He countered with telling me that my constant quest for the truth kept the issue, when he had clearly made the right decision and come home.

I was supposed to reward him for choosing me. *Be grateful that I have options, but I chose you.* The problem came when I no longer felt like he was a prize. The more he embarrassed me with his constant search for friendship with other women, the less exciting football games became. I stopped wearing his jersey or making shirts that showed my support. I became afraid. I worried the day would come when I would look into the crowd and see a girl who looked like me proudly sporting his number.

A week after the $60 restaurant charge, I logged on to Facebook, and my trusty informant had been tagged in pictures with the girl Robert was seeing. Their group of friends posted a picture of their freshly painted toenails. The caption, comments, and interaction all implied that they were a sisterhood. Now I really didn't know whom to trust. The more they exchanged inside jokes on their Facebook walls and statuses, the more I believed Robert. I had confided in this woman, and now I felt like she had betrayed me, fed me the words her true friend wanted me to hear. I imagined they spent the evening laughing at how they had gotten one over on me.

So I buried the secret in my heart and placed the wall around my heart. I knew we were a long way from being okay.

And then a few weeks later, I stood before God, my parents, siblings, family, and friends and asked for their blessing over my mess. I didn't shed one tear walking down the aisle because I knew I wasn't marrying the man I wanted to spend the rest of my life with. I was marrying the boy I prayed would become that man.

Isn't it incredible the messes we get ourselves into and then ask God to clean up? I prayed every day from the moment we got married to finally feel safe. I wanted to know what it felt like to have a home again. I wanted to be afraid that something had happened to my husband when he wasn't home on time. Instead, the panic was not about his safety, but for the next heartbreak I'd have to brace for.

It wasn't just the fact that Robert had four children he forgot to mention to me that made me call Dr. Nicole. It was that I was beginning to feel like the problem was too big for me to handle on my own anymore. I wanted to protect him from my parents' scrutiny, so I never said a word.

I would protect him even if he wasn't protecting me.

I gave selfless love to a selfish person and he emptied me out. I had nothing left. I couldn't feel anything anymore, nor did I want to. I didn't want to face the feeling my heart had each time I heard a new name. Like physical pain palpating my soul. He hurt me over and over again. The aching became normal and there were no more tears left to cry. I bled for him. Poured my soul out. Tried to fill him up. He was the only addiction I've ever had. He lifted me up and then dropped me into a thousand different pieces. Each time he gave me hope, I was on cloud nine, addicted to the lie that we would be all right.

I knew I wasn't marrying the man I wanted to spend the rest of my life with. I was marrying the boy I prayed would become that man.

And as silly as it must seem that I stayed, even knowing what I was getting myself into, I knew I was not alone. We silence our voice because after you've stayed through so much, you can't walk away without facing the questions. "What was the final straw?" they would want to know. "You finally got tired," they would say. I was afraid that leaving would make me more insecure than staying. Because no matter how many women there had been, he always came home. All roads led back to me. Leaving meant admitting that I wasn't enough for him. I wasn't ready to leave him to the women his actions already displayed that truth to.

He put a hole in my heart, and no matter how I tried to patch it with the fake confidence of knowing at the end of the day he's mine, I still felt the leaking. Not one day passed when I didn't think about how I was losing. I had been wounded time after time, and trying to walk without a limp each day became my task. My best friend since fifteen, Stacia, knew more than anyone, and even she didn't know it all. She never tried to force me to leave or talk badly about him. Instead, she got on the other side of me and helped me patch the wounds.

Stacia called me strong. I felt so weak.

Until we decide that our time, love, and heart have been invested and will not yield a return, we stay. No one wants to gamble his or her last and lose. I wanted to win. I wanted to be right about him. Ultimately I should have been teaching myself the lesson I so badly wanted him to learn. I wanted him to value me, but how could I teach him my value if I accepted everything, even the pain, he gave me?

I tried to become more confident, because he told me that my insecurity was what attracted women to him. I stopped talking about how hurt I was because he told me I was rubbing his past in his face. Or that I was self-inflicting the pain because I refused to let things go. You should never have to be with someone who wants you to be his or her robot. You were created to feel, and anyone who tries to control how you feel is trying to become your master—and when you let him or her do that, you become his or her slave.

I wanted Dr. Nicole to help me be free in my own home. Maybe she could help us find a way to level the playing field so we could see and embrace each other fully. The first couple of sessions weren't easy. We both had to take responsibility for the things that had hurt each other.

How could I expect God

to correct my marriage

if I was constantly trying

to do the job for Him?

Even though I felt justified in saying the things that hurt him, the truth is that I still let him control my character. I tried to use my words to make him feel the weight his betrayal had placed on my heart. Maybe if I cut him deep enough he would see what it felt like to bleed, too. I apologized, though, because I wanted to have a whole husband, not a wounded little boy.

How could I expect God to correct my marriage if I was constantly trying to do the job for Him? Robert wanted to control me and I wanted to control him. Our war was tearing each other apart. In the presence of our peacemaker, Dr. Nicole, we waved the white flag. Because of that moment, our marriage took a turn for the better.

When two people become one before God, we no longer just represent ourselves; we represent one another. Therefore, you can no longer offer your wounded mate to Him without recognizing that you're wounded, too. I knew that I had been hurt, but I thought if he changed I would be okay. I prayed that God would show me how I could get his heart, but I placed a wall around my own.

Until we strengthened our own walks with Christ, we couldn't be much help to each other. We committed to going to service every Sunday. There would be days we fought the entire way to church, but there was something about being in the presence of God that moved our flesh out of the way and allowed our souls an opportunity to connect.

Despite our drama, Robert was more focused on school and football than he had ever been. It was his senior year, and if he didn't stand out academically and athletically, life after college would be hard. His dream of playing in the NFL was drawing closer, soon to be within his grasp. Being drafted by a professional football team not only would improve our finances dramatically, but it would be a huge personal validation for Robert as an athlete and as a man.

Although I was still working with the air force contractor, I no longer had the passion I once did. Most of the planes had been sent to Iraq, and we weren't expecting a new fleet for quite some time. Still, I continued to work on improving the filing system, organization, and procedures for our contracts. When any of the guys were scheduled to fly out, I made their travel arrangements, created itineraries, and endeavored to make sure they didn't return to unnecessary work. After my first evaluation, I received a raise. I called Robert first and then my parents and told them the news.

The next day my dad offered me a job. I turned in my notice immediately.

I had spent most of my life wanting to work for my father and almost two years accepting that I would never get the opportunity. Then, when I least expected, the door opened. My dad saw something in me that I was just learning to see myself.

In the moment, it felt like God was honoring our commitment to at least try to become better. Robert was excelling on the football field. I was finally helping my father in a field more interesting than accounting. I was brought on to help structure grassroots marketing for our first film with Sony Pictures.

So often we look for Him to calm the storms of our lives. But there are times when the storm can't go away because we need the rain.

As with most lessons in life, I know now that working with my father wasn't only a validation of my test of faith. It was God getting me closer to the people I would need more than ever in due time. There are no coincidences with God. At the time I reveled at the grace He showed me even though I had strayed so far from Him.

When God chooses to trust us with grace, it's because He believes that we're capable of doing things better than we did before.

Merciful God that He is, He doesn't just leave us in our misery to suffer. When we learn to find peace in trial, He knows that our season of suffering can come to an end. So often we look for Him to calm the storms of our lives. But there are times when the storm can't go away because we need the rain.

Can you stop being afraid of the thunder long enough to feel the rain?

With certain struggles, when you get the lesson, the struggle is no longer necessary. If the struggle continues, the lesson has not been learned. God doesn't need us to have perfect lives, just willing ones. Are you willing to move your pride out of the way?

I was trying. As much as my trust with Robert had eroded, I made a commitment to do better. I wanted to believe that he was holding up his end of the bargain, but I could no longer focus on him. I needed to heal. If I wanted to have a healthy marriage, my healing was the only thing I had control over.

We get so caught up in trying to nurse our loved ones back to health that we forget about ourselves. You can be everything to everyone and nothing to yourself. Or you can choose to teach others how to take care of themselves by leading by example. When your love doesn't seem to be enough for them, try using it to love on yourself. Every once in a while, you have to remind yourself that you're important, too. You can't depend on those around you to know when you're running low on hope, or to recognize that you can't give what you don't have.

As much as I wanted Robert to believe in our love, if I'm completely honest, I never truly believed in the love we had either, just the love we were capable of achieving. I didn't want to live like that any longer. I accepted that I couldn't change him, but I could use the drop of hope I had left to become better myself.

It seemed like the more I worked on myself, the closer he and I became. I wasn't playing detective or snooping in his stuff. I treated him like the husband I wanted him to become, not the one who had hurt me. When Thanksgiving came around, we were stronger than we had ever been, period. Despite our troubles, we had so much for which to be grateful. We were growing and making progress.

We were excited because my parents were taking us to Mexico for the holiday. Since Robert had practice, we wouldn't leave until Wednesday, but my son went ahead with my parents earlier in the week. Then the day we were scheduled to leave, we got a call. Robert couldn't get a passport. Evidently, when you are in arrears on child support, you can't leave the country. I was devastated. I'd never been away from my family during the holidays.

When my mother heard the news, she strongly suggested I come anyway. I could tell she had finally had enough of the lies and disappointment. I knew she was just upset that we wouldn't all be together, so I let her finish her speech. When she was done, I asked her what she would do if it were Daddy. That ended our conversation.

A month later I learned I was pregnant.

I was concerned over the way Robert related, or didn't, with his children back in east Texas. Still, I had a life inside of me, I was married, and I was working. We would have to deal with everything else as it came.

And boy did it come. Robert didn't pass enough classes to play in the bowl game for TCU. We watched the news of his class failure scroll across the screen. No game meant no exposure at the time NFL scouts and agents were looking the most. This was their chance to see how the players performed under pressure and outside of their own environment. The only thing they would know about Robert was that he didn't do what was necessary to make his way onto the field. He had worked so hard, and now the dream seemed to be slipping through his fingers.

We were devastated, but a part of me was secretly glad. Maybe without football he would become more focused on maturing. I wanted his dream to come true, but I knew Robert had a problem. The celebrity lifestyle that came with college ball would only intensify when you added big money and even more national exposure to the equation. Still, I knew that so much of his self-esteem was riding on whether or not he could play football at the next level. In the end, I prayed that God's will would be done. I just wish I had asked Him for the strength to handle whatever it was.

We had to wait over three months between the bowl game Robert missed and the NFL draft in April. During that time he talked to several scouts, a couple of agents, and friends who had turned pro, and they all thought he still had a chance. But even if chosen by a professional team, Robert would still have a lot to prove. Getting drafted was just the first step in a whole new system where he would be required to start over and prove himself once again.

Draft week finally arrived, and it felt like we were all holding our breath. There are seven rounds in the NFL draft. Each team receives seven opportunities to add talent to their team. We were hoping Robert would be drafted, but we knew it was more likely he would get the chance to walk on a team as a free agent. At the time, the draft was held over two days: Saturday (rounds 1–4) and Sunday (rounds 5–7). We knew that if Robert got drafted it would be on Sunday afternoon, so we went to church in the morning, then came home to wait for news.

I was five months pregnant at the time. I'm powerless against a good Sunday nap, even without a child in my womb. I don't even know when I fell asleep, but I remember waking up to Robert busting into the family room.

"Yes, sir. I'm ready to play ball!"

10

Playing Games

ROBERT WAS OFFICIALLY going to get his shot at the next level. I was happy for him. His dream had finally come true, but would mine?

Life in the NFL scared me.

It offered the next level of achievement for Robert, but I suspected it would also bring new, unexpected challenges. Or maybe they weren't so unexpected, but I tried to bury them in the end zone under the stadium lights. My biggest fear was that the safety we had created over the last few months would be shattered. We were finally drama free. No women, no issues, just us. I prayed and prayed that the promotion wouldn't change him back to the person who had made me build the walls.

After the draft, the text messages flooded our phones for days. People congratulated Robert and asked how long we'd be in Texas so that they could see us off before we headed to Virginia, where the team's training facility was located, to join the Redskins. Gratefully,

I gave God credit for it all. But when I laid my head down at night, I couldn't find the words to silence my insecurities. How do you handle the tension when God's blessing makes you afraid?

How do you handle the tension when God's blessing makes you afraid?

Proverbs 10:22 tells us, "The blessing of the Lord makes one rich, and He adds no sorrow with it" (NKJV). Here I was married to an official NFL player, and I couldn't help but feel like I was on the edge of a cliff. I was pregnant and would have to leave my entire family to stand by my man in D.C.—the same man I wasn't sure would be standing beside me. We knew all along that this could be a possibility, moving away to play for a pro team, having a baby together, but when the moment actually arrived, it felt different.

Be careful what you ask for.

I was being plucked from my roots and being trusted to establish new ones. In early May Robert had to start rookie camp and begin competing for a spot as a middle linebacker and special teams member on the final roster. Even though he had been drafted, it didn't guarantee that he would make the team's final cut of only fifty-three players. Given how unlikely we thought his being drafted would be, I knew that we'd both have to be strong and secure enough for him to focus.

When he left for Virginia, I moved into my parents' home but continued to pay rent on the apartment so as not to break the lease. The plan was for Robert to fly back to Dallas on weekends when possible, and then toward the end of the summer, once we had a better idea whether he would make the team, I would join him in Virginia. In the meantime, I wanted to soak up as much of my parents' wisdom

Doing the right thing will

make you better,

but it doesn't make life

any easier.

as possible. I just wish I had known that there would be a day when even it would not be enough to console me.

If I could travel back in time and leave a note for myself, I would simply say this: *Despite how it feels, you'll be okay.* It probably wouldn't have made much sense to anyone on the outside to whisper that to me. After all, I was living the dream. I should just step up and do the right thing, enjoy all that we were being given, and stop worrying about all that could go wrong.

Knowing what I had to do didn't provide any comfort. There's this old wives' tale we hear and start believing at a young age, that doing the right thing will make you feel good. The truth is, doing the right thing will make you better, but it doesn't make life any easier. If I had done only what felt good, I would've stayed in my parents' house, where I would have help with the baby and support for when I felt like I was breaking.

But my husband told me he wanted me to be with him. He was my family now. So I put on my big girl shoes and rose to the occasion not knowing how difficult the next steps on our journey would be.

So whenever I would feel the chill of fear surround my heart, I tried to break it down. It reminded me of my bad habit of eating ice. I wouldn't even wait for the drink to be gone before I started digging for the ice. When I heard somewhere that eating ice helps you burn calories, I vowed to never stop. My addiction became so bad, I would sit in my car during the summer and blast the heat while I ate ice. It didn't happen all at once, but once the ice started melting from being in my mouth, it became soft enough for me to use my teeth. Before I knew it, one piece was gone and I was working on the next one.

If I could melt my fears little by little the same way, maybe I would survive. Maybe by joining my husband, despite the fear, I would be able to melt a little bit of the anxiety. When I worried about my pregnancy, I reminded myself to pray and trust God with our future. Little by little, I began to release some of the stress generated by my imagination.

It was a kind of turning point for me. I realized that maturity requires learning enough about yourself to identify the emotions you feel and why. I had to dig deeper than just whether I was doing okay in the moment or having a bad day. I couldn't just walk around always on the verge of an emotional explosion without knowing the ingredients generating such combustion.

I learned we have to be able to connect the dots that create the image of who we are in order to pinpoint exactly what's wrong and fix it. Surgeons rarely operate blindly, if they can help it. Sometimes they get several different angles of the same area, just to be sure they know exactly what's going on. You have to know how something was broken before you can determine the best way to fix it. I was determined to keep facing down my fears.

We have to be able to connect the dots that create the image of who we are in order to pinpoint exactly what's wrong and fix it.

Once I realized why I was afraid, the only thing I could do to outrun the feeling was to do the opposite. I tried to be courageous when I felt the most afraid, but I wasn't sure if that actually made me brave or just foolish. Still, I thought pretending would give my heart the CPR it needed to believe again.

During those weeks Robert and I were apart, I made the most of the time with my parents. On the weekends, Mom and I cooked, shopped, or indulged in our favorite pastime of taking naps. She and I had become friends, drawing closer through these new chapters in my married life. Leaving them would be so hard, especially since we were developing such a deeper, stronger relationship.

But I was comforted knowing that my mother and close family friend—we call her Aunt April—would accompany me on my first visit to see Robert, since it was definitely looking like he would make the team. The training facility for the Redskins was in Ashburn, Virginia, about thirty-five minutes from Washington, D.C. We were going to tour the hospital, look for doctors, and find a home Robert and I could rent until we knew for sure whether the area would be home. Then we would all return so I could finish up loose ends back in Texas before returning to Virginia indefinitely.

A few days before my trip, my father took me into my parents' room. I crawled onto their bed to get off my feet with my swollen stomach. He kneeled beside me with tears in his eyes.

"I don't want you to go," he whispered, "but I know you're doing the right thing."

"I'm scared, Daddy," I said. "But you're right, it is the right thing for me."

"I'm scared, too," he said. "But God will take care of you."

I appreciated that he was respecting me as an adult woman, not his little girl anymore. But I also understood something about how powerless he must've felt. What do you do when you're incapable of protecting your child anymore? How do you pacify someone when you're afraid yourself?

We want solutions, but the older you get, the more you realize that some choices aren't win or lose. As a matter of fact, they become some twisted version of both joy and pressure. You buy a house, but you also get a mortgage. You get into school, but how will you afford it?

So often life gives us the chance to be happy on one end and completely afraid on the other. Those are the struggles that come with being blessed. The blessing itself adds no sorrow, but the way it creates your new normal changes everything.

I wished for a crystal ball and a YouTube video on how to use it, because I wanted so badly to prepare for the road ahead. Everything was so uncertain before me, but I didn't have the time to waver in my decision. If I waited too long, I would be too far into my pregnancy to travel.

All I could do was ask God for the strength and wisdom to handle whatever waited around the corner.

Once in D.C., we toured the hospital and met my new doctor. The Redskins' Realtor showed us a few homes that were available for rent. While my mother and Aunt April stayed at a nearby hotel, I opted to stay with Robert in the housing the team provided for us so I could see him when his training day was over. His training camp roommate and his girlfriend, Simone, were both from Texas, and she happened to come up at the same time I was there. So the two of us went to dinner and watched TV together in the apartment.

Simone and I instantly connected. Their college was known for churning out professional football players, so they had an idea of what the lifestyle would be like. Most of the players Robert and I knew were league veterans, on their way toward or already in retirement. It was nice to have someone who understood the nerves and excitement of transitioning to this new stage.

The night I was scheduled to return to Dallas and finish packing before returning to D.C. for good, my back began aching. Initially, I thought it was due to the traveling and running around town. When I started having cold sweats and a fever, I told my mom I needed to go to the hospital. They admitted me immediately. I had a kidney infection, a common but serious complication in pregnancy.

I had been treated for the same thing in Texas twice before coming to Virginia, although I'd never had to be admitted to the hospital. Robert was still training and couldn't afford to be by my side for every moment, so my mom stayed with me. I was there for five days before the doctors released me. There was one stipulation, though: I could not fly back home as planned.

We had only looked at potential homes on our visit. I wasn't prepared to move so suddenly. My mom changed her flight. She was going to help me figure everything out. My dad was on his way, too.

My income wouldn't cover our rent back home in addition to the unexpected costs of moving into our new home. Robert had been drafted, but he didn't actually have a check yet. So once we found a place, my parents loaned us the money and helped us move in. My dad and Robert spent the day hanging window blinds in the new house.

Mom, Aunt April, and I went shopping for necessities: cleaning supplies, towels, bed frame, and mattress. They tried to make me as comfortable as possible under the circumstances. When everything was set up, Robert had to leave for practice and my family had to catch their flight. No matter how short we tried to make our good-byes, there was no denying that it felt like my family and I were being ripped from one another.

I closed the door and accessed a new level on my journey of becoming a wife. I was going to have to do this without my mom and dad there to save me. Sure, they were just a flight away, but they had their own lives. When I wanted to call them for support, I would have to reserve it for when I needed them the most.

Which felt like only a few hours after they had flown out of D.C. That first night in our newly set up home, I got a text from Robert saying that he was going to stay at his dorm-style apartment near the training facility. Since cable had not been installed in our house yet, he was going to remain in his room there. I didn't have a car, and the trip was too far for him to come and get me, especially given my condition.

So I spent the first night in our new house alone. It would not be my last.

––––––

At my follow-up appointment with the doctor a few days later, I begged her to let me go home once my body could handle it. It was still only May, and I wasn't due until August. I hadn't even had my baby shower yet. I needed to get back to Dallas. My doctor saw the desperation in my eyes. She obliged and told me as long as I didn't have any further incidents I would be fine. But she wanted me to wait at least another week or two before flying to make sure I remained stabilized.

The following week, when Robert received his signing bonus and the cable was finally installed, I went shopping to finish furnishing the house. I wanted to make our home somewhere he'd be proud to come. I knew how he had grown up, and I remembered our days in our old apartment. There was clearly more going on with him than he was letting on, and I knew it was bigger than having ESPN on all the time. I felt like he wanted to be a bachelor again and that his pregnant wife had cramped his style. But when rookie camp ended and the player housing was no longer available, he finally seemed grateful to come home.

Robert was never selfish with money. When our anniversary came around, he went all out: designer purse, weekend getaway, diamonds, romantic dinner, and horse and carriage rides. I held on to my hope that maybe he was maturing and settling into married life. Before he bought anything for himself, he showered me with gifts. He told me that I had taken care of us for so long, now it was his time.

We settled into Virginia life and flew back to Texas only once. Robert's break between camps came in early July, and my doctor had given the okay for me to travel for my baby shower back home. At my last doctor's appointment before training camp began—when Robert would have to leave again—the doctor told me that I was definitely going to have the baby early. I called my mom excited, because I knew she'd come. Robert left for camp, and my mom and youngest brother, Dexter, came up.

Those were the best weeks of my life. I imagined that it was a taste of what a normal life would have been. No one was coming by the house to see if it was where the Jakes family lived. A few people recognized my mom, but for the most part we got to be regular people. I gained more weight during the time my mom was there than in my whole pregnancy. We took turns cooking breakfast, lunch, and dinner every day. We barbecued and met the neighbors. Malachi even made new friends at a summer camp around the corner.

It was the calm before the storm.

Robert had very few off days during training camp, so we asked the doctor to induce my labor when he could be there for the birth. After over twelve hours in labor, I welcomed our daughter, Makenzie, on August 14, 2009. She shared her middle name with my mother and her birthday with Dexter.

Makenzie was not the only new girl in Robert's life. I found out about the other one a week after giving birth. Robert had an off day and was allowed to come home and stay the night. In the middle of feeding Makenzie, I flipped through our phone bill. I saw the same number over and over. It looked like he'd called me each night and then immediately called this other number.

While he was sleeping I called this number, blocking my own. A woman answered, her voice hoarse from sleep. I immediately hung up. Makenzie was finally sleeping, but there was no way I could. The emotional tide of my fresh maternity wounds swept over me and tears poured from my eyes.

Then I learned they had been texting each other throughout the time I was in labor as well. I remembered how Robert had prayed over me when the doctor prepped me for my cesarean. New tears burned my face. I could contain myself no longer.

"Who is she?" I ripped the blankets away from his peaceful slumber.

"What?" he said and sat up, immediately clued in to my distress. "Who? What are you talking about?"

I shoved the phone records in his face. "Who is she?" I repeated, trying to regain control of myself.

"Just calm down, baby. She's just a promoter," he said. "We were strategizing how to make the fans more aware of my presence on the team."

I eyed him suspiciously. Was I overreacting?

"It's strictly work related," he said. "Just ask her."

Frantically, I began to compose text after text, hitting send each time. Minutes passed and no response. I was going to have to believe him again, at least until she responded.

"You think I would pray over you and then text my mistress?" he asked.

I let it go. My body couldn't handle the stress of fighting, and I didn't want the baby to wake up. Maybe my emotions were being jacked up by all the hormones in my body. Maybe I really was out of line to accuse him.

The woman didn't text me back, and I didn't bring it up again. Two weeks later, Robert was informed he'd made the team. I was happy for him and depressed for me. Nothing had really changed for us. And now we had a daughter to raise.

Over the course of that football season, there would be four more women he hid from me. He saved their numbers in his phone under teammates' names, and even got another cell phone so that it was no longer on our shared bill. When I asked him about it, he lied and told me all the rookies had a special phone in case the veterans needed something.

The next day I asked Simone if this were true. She looked at me with compassion in her eyes and didn't say a word. She didn't have to say anything. Her silence was louder than her words.

When football season ended, I told Robert I wanted to go back to Dallas. So we packed our bags and moved back to my parents' home. Perhaps being around family would help us find our way again. Of all the girls that had come and gone in the short time we were in Virginia, the "promoter" was the most consistent.

One evening when the voices in my head were too loud to ignore, I tried to text her again. I told her that I knew she probably wouldn't reply, but I had a family and a heart and I needed to know the truth.

My phone rang immediately and my heart jumped into my throat.

"Thank you," I said softly, answering the phone. "Tell me the truth."

She told me everything. She'd been in our home when I had gone back to visit family. Robert often came to her house. They'd had sex more times than she wanted to share. She told me that I wouldn't believe the things he said about me. I asked her for something specific, and all she could say was, "It's not good."

As if God knew that the pain was going to wash over me, my mother came in and saw the tears streaming down my face and immediately grabbed the phone from my hand. I had been working for her since returning from Virginia; after an employee left the ministry unexpectedly, she asked if I would help her. I didn't know if she had come over to talk about work or if she was just checking on us, but the timing was divine.

She spoke something into the phone and then left the room. I couldn't hear what was being said over my own tears, but before I knew it, Robert was sitting in front of me admitting that he'd had an affair.

The next morning I got in my car and headed to work. I was numb. My mother and I had not talked yet. I still hadn't uttered a word about the previous night to anyone. Turning on music to drown the thoughts in my head, I found a song that I knew would say the words I couldn't.

Comparing love to a hurricane, Jazmine Sullivan crooned my heartbreak and I cried fresh tears. I cried for the girl who knew all along that this day was coming. I cried for the walls I'd built that didn't protect me from this searing pain. I cried for pieces of myself I had buried in the name of love. I lost my joy, my peace, my hope, and my belief in a love that wasn't worth fighting for.

This war was almost over, but I wasn't sure if I was winning or losing.

Or both.

I cried every day. I played the song until the words ripped off the bandage and made me bleed again. I let the pain wash over me. I gave in.

I called my friend Stacia, and all I could do was cry more. I heard her sniffle in my ear, and together we held a memorial for the parts of me I missed. No matter how many tears fell, I knew that when my eyes were dry the pain would still be there.

I didn't say anything to Robert. I didn't have the words. I didn't want to hear his apology or even his excuses. One of the Redskins veteran wives called to tell me about a conference for professional athletes, and they wanted to sponsor Robert and me. The conference just happened to be taking place in Dallas. Robert must've pleaded with God for it to be there, because there was no way I would be going away with him.

We went to the conference and wept as a couple. Surrounded by men who struggled and overcame the same issues, Robert committed to trying to make us work. We attended church and counseling in Dallas until off-season training began that spring. Per the suggestion of our counselor, Robert would return to Virginia alone. During that time he was to find and attend counseling. It was the only way I would go back, the only way I could even consider trying to forgive him yet again.

He did his part, so I returned to our home in Virginia that summer of 2010. I wasn't hopeful, but I didn't have the strength to end our marriage—or to save it. We attended counseling together for a while, but the conversations reached dead ends.

Nonetheless, Robert attempted to rebuild our connection. He wasn't staying out all night. He helped with the kids and seemed committed to fixing the broken bond between us. Before we knew it, training camp was starting again and he would once again be competing for a spot on the roster. The coaching staff had experienced some changes, so Robert would have to step up and prove himself all over again.

In the August preseason games, the more experienced players often start before the coaches let the ones trying to prove themselves finish the second half. That's when the guys who are right on the bubble get a chance to show what they have. Robert was having a tremendous preseason and had all but solidified his spot on the team. He was one of the leaders in preseason tackles, and the sports columnists speculated he'd be a great backup to their seasoned veteran.

As part of our honor system, I continued to check our phone bill and was yet to find anything suspicious since the last bombshell. Then one day Robert told me that one of his teammates had used

Robert's phone to call his girlfriend; I should ignore any new numbers I spotted. He erased the number out of his call log to respect his friend's privacy. I knew where this was headed.

Sure enough, whenever I walked into the room, he would rush to end his calls. At night he just happened to fall asleep with his phone in his pillowcase. Then we received a welcome letter in the mail from a cell phone carrier other than our own. I asked him, he denied it. The letter came by accident, he explained.

"You should trust me by now," he said. "We can't get better if you don't believe I'm telling you the truth."

Two days before the last preseason game—an away game—Robert came home to have dinner and grab some things for his trip. He came in through the front door instead of the garage, which I thought was strange. He immediately ran upstairs to gather his things. We weren't talking much since the recent suspicions I carried.

Looking out the window, I saw the taillights of his car about a block down our street. I knew as I opened the front door and took the steps toward the car that it wasn't going to be good.

And there she was. . . .

In the passenger seat of his car, waiting on him to come back so they could leave, sat a young woman. When she looked up and saw me, she just grinned. She didn't ask me who I was or seem surprised to see me standing in front of her.

"WHAT ARE YOU DOING WITH MY HUSBAND?" I yelled. A fresh supply of rage fueled my question. I didn't care who heard me, what would happen, or how she responded. The last straw had already tipped the scales, and yet Robert continued to heap on a stack of last straws.

"WE KICKIN' IT!" she said defiantly, clearly annoyed by my question.

Before I could show her what happens to people who kick it with other people's husbands, Robert came running out of the house.

"I'm just taking her home—she's my homeboy's friend," he tried to explain.

I looked at him, wondering just how foolish he thought I really was.

"There's nothing going on," he continued. "I don't even know her."

I didn't say a word but turned back to the house. He trailed behind me pleading his case. I grabbed my keys and headed to the basement, where I could access the garage. He grabbed me. I was unable to move. I hit him as hard as I could in his stomach, but still he was stronger than me. I kept fighting. Fighting to be free from him, from this, from our poisonous love. I didn't want to love him. I didn't want to live like this anymore. I was tired of tasting the salt of my tears. I was tired of building this white picket fence that he was intent on burning down.

He held me until my blows were too hard and he had no choice but to let me go. I said everything I ever wanted to say to him. I addressed his poor parenting, his lack of integrity, and his immorality. Calling him a boy would've been a compliment; he was less than that to me. I used every curse word I could find, and when those ran out I made up new ones.

Then I grabbed my keys, hopped into my car, and backed out of the garage. I pulled up behind his car and started ramming it over and over again while his latest conquest finally realized she should be scared.

Now in his car, Robert sped down the road of our residential neighborhood. I followed behind them, before quickly realizing that I would have to go back home. My children were sleeping, oblivious to the hurricane taking place both outside and within their home. Then we both stopped. I saw him grab his phone. I grabbed mine and took pictures of the two of them in the car, then turned to go home.

It was too late, though; he had called the police on me.

The officer met me outside our house. When the officer finally approached me, he asked what was going on.

"My husband brought his girlfriend to our house. I had a problem with that."

I heard the words but didn't recognize the voice.

So this was what it felt like to be driven crazy, literally. To lose it so fast you didn't even know who you were anymore. The officer let me go with a warning and told Robert, who had just come up behind us, to leave for the night. The policeman clearly felt sorry for me, and I could see it in his eyes. I couldn't bear to see his pity any longer. I took his papers, promised to visit with Child Protective Services and a social worker, and went inside.

Two nights later I watched the away game with the other wives, each of us holding in our own secrets. Robert was having an incredible game. He was heading into the double digits for tackles when a defensive lineman landed on his knee. Robert didn't get up; he couldn't move. The cameras followed him wobbling off the field and onto the sideline. The announcers speculated on the injury and replayed the video over and over. The other wives attempted to console me, but I assured them I was fine.

The game had been over for an hour when I heard the buzz of the other wives' phones. Their husbands were checking in, but Robert didn't bother to call. It was during the post-game show that I learned he'd torn his meniscus.

There wouldn't be any more football for him.

There wouldn't be any more injuries for me.

The games had finally ended.

11

Every Ending
Is a New Beginning

IT'S EASY TO blame my heartbreak on him, but no one was more responsible than I was.

I had been disappointed when I got pregnant at thirteen and gave birth at fourteen. I was upset when I dropped out of college. I tried so long not to be a statistic, but the expectations were too much and I quit. I didn't want to be a disappointment to myself again, a quitter, someone who couldn't keep fighting for her marriage. I didn't want to risk failing again, so I stayed with someone who expected nothing from me while I expected everything from him. I thought that by exceeding his nonexistent expectations I would inspire him to attempt to meet at least some of mine.

It was as if I was intent on speaking Italian when all he could understand was Spanish. My language never reached his ears because he didn't want to learn the vocabulary required to understand the message of my love. I had foolishly assumed that with love came loyalty and respect. But those three are so distinct that it's a disservice to bundle them all together within four little letters. I had never accepted love that didn't come with loyalty. I couldn't understand it and this upset me. I was mad at him for not speaking the language of love that he'd never bothered to learn. I hadn't experienced enough to understand that sometimes too much is lost in translation. Both people have to want to communicate to create their conversation.

> *Both people have to want to communicate to create their conversation.*

Perhaps this explains why love will always be one of the hardest words to define. Its meaning is so relative. My grandmother once told my father, "When falling in love, never go first," warning that the one who falls first assumes all the risk. However, based on my experience, I would update her advice to say, "When falling in love, never go alone."

I had fallen head over heels into earth-shattering love. I just didn't realize how low it was going to take me. I found myself beyond the dirt where the seeds of our love should've made the world more fruitful. No, our love dragged us down to the hottest layer of the earth, to the molten core where nothing survives without being charred. Our love made tears that served no purpose. We had burned through years of our lives with passion, anger, and pain.

I wanted my marriage to be my safe place, my refuge. Yet with each incident of another woman, lie, and betrayal it became the inferno from which I could never escape. The girl in me who liked to chew ice had melted away, leaving nothing but a puddle of who I once was.

Finally, I was ready to transform my pain into wisdom, my tears into fuel for change. I had learned so much the hard way. Allow me to tell you what I said to myself during those days when I was trying to find the strength to get on my feet and walk out the door.

You want to believe that love conquers all. It's what they tell us. That if we love someone enough, nothing else will matter. The truth is love isn't enough if it makes you worse. Love is far too sweet to have left you so bitter.

You're strong enough to want more. You're better than this moment. And believe it or not, even if, like me, you wasted into nothing, know that your mess is a beautiful blank canvas for Him.

You must be willing to admit that you have lost your way and can't escape the pain. Open your mouth and ask for help. Be willing to admit that you were wrong. That you're broken and you're afraid of doing it on your own. Each time you give your fear a voice, it can no longer whisper into your destiny. The Enemy is counting on us to give in. He wants us to lose our way.

Don't let him win.

So no matter what rumors they may tell, or worse, what truth may spread, it's not worth your being this person you don't recognize. It's not worth missing out on your purpose. The more you can be distracted by things and people, the less time you have to search and find what God has placed inside of you.

> *Love isn't enough if it makes you worse. Love is far too sweet to have left you so bitter.*

We say we have no talent. We tell them we don't fit. We talk ourselves out of a tomorrow because we are afraid to let go of today. Give yourself the permission to heal, to be restored, and to be redeemed. You don't have to be punished anymore. You don't have to be that person crying, screaming, hurting, doubting, writhing in agony because someone else won't love you the way you want them to.

I could not change Robert. I could not love him enough to change. Only Robert could ever love himself enough to change.

I thought of his children we saw maybe twice a year, usually at my suggestion. I thought of his sister, who challenged him not to forget where he came from. I thought of his mother, who always said she wished he'd come home more often. I think Ms. Samantha eventually realized that I was not the one keeping him from visiting her.

The more you can be distracted by things and people, the less time you have to search and find what God has placed inside of you.

When Robert finally called me the morning after his injury, the first thing he said was, "Guess this is what I deserve, huh?" I didn't even take the opportunity to gloat. What difference would it make? It didn't change that we were two people killing each other little by little. I asked him what the plan was for his knee. He didn't know that my bags were packed and the kids and I were going back to Texas. He was going to have surgery the next day.

"I know you're not going to want to take care of me, but I don't have anyone else." He wanted to see if we could convince his mother to fly in. When I talked to Ms. Samantha, she was adamantly against it at first, since she'd never flown before. Then she relented and said she'd come when she could. I agreed to postpone my trip and at least get him through surgery.

The recovery process wasn't easy. To top it off, Robert was still sneaking around with the same girl he had brought to the house. I'm ashamed to say it, but I finally managed to get her number out

What we create

is what we're

responsible for,

not what we wanted.

of his phone. I texted her the lies he was telling me. She told me that she knew what was real. I asked her to come over and take care of him so I could leave. She told me that Robert wasn't lying to me and that the two of them really weren't together. I told her that she wasn't the first one. I listed over a dozen names and sent them to her. She laughed at me. I tried to upset her, thinking she would then tell me the truth.

As much as I didn't want to change my definition of love, marriage, and relationships, what we create is what we're responsible for, not what we wanted. We say we want to lose weight, but then we eat the worst possible things. We say we want to save money, but then we buy the TV on sale at Target. We say we want to be better, but we stay in situations that make us worse. If nothing changes, then nothing changes. I continued to repeat the same vicious cycle of love, but I was dying for more.

What are you willing to sacrifice on the quest for God's will? Are you willing to give up on what you want, how you want it, and when you want it? Or are you so obsessed with having everything right now that He stops fighting with you? God let me have my way. He gave me everything I asked for, and it all tore me apart. I had a successful husband, a beautiful home, amazing children, and a wonderful family. It just didn't seem as pretty anymore once I finally got it.

I thought that God was breaking Robert, teaching him that if he treated me the way he did, he'd no longer be able to live his dream: *"Until you take care of what I've given you, I won't add to it."* I was believing in God for him, but who was believing in Him for me? My parents could have guessed, but they didn't know how badly I was breaking. They didn't know how much I was hurting.

Now I know that Robert's knee was just a reflection of my walk with God. I took on the weight of something too big for me to handle and tore under the pressure. Even after the surgery, his behavior didn't stop. The Redskins placed him on the injured reserve list, so his workdays were much shorter. He couldn't even be on the sidelines during practice or games. He was watching his dream from the outside looking in because he was too hurt to play.

We both were.

I watched the other wives, who seemed to have it all together. Their eyes had so much more life in them than mine. Occasionally, there would be that one wife whose face was a reflection of my own. We locked eyes, nodded our heads, and smiled to the rest of the team, but we knew. We knew we were living a lie.

There's this misconception that once you make it to a certain place in life, you escape all problems and trouble. We were young, well-known, and financially secure, but we were also exhausted, angry, and emotionally bankrupt. I stopped calling home. I couldn't fake any sign of joy. I stopped caring whether the dishes were done or dinner was cooked when Robert got home. I stopped giving him love he didn't deserve. And I know that that pushed him further to *her*, but I couldn't do it anymore. I couldn't pretend like this was okay. We were roommates.

I remember when Robert got released to drive; I knew we would have problems. At some point during his recovery, I finally found the spare phone that he was hiding from me. When I picked it up, even with his knee still freshly wounded, he chased me down the hall. I put the phone in the washing machine and turned it on. He wasn't even upset that the phone was ruined, as long as I couldn't see what was on it. In the heat of one of our arguments about him, her, the affair/not affair, he tried to make me feel like I was crazy. I told Robert I was going home. He told me he'd have her things in my closet before my plane took off.

We have these times when we're tired of being the bigger person. Eventually, we decide to treat people the way they treat us. I felt the anger turning my heart black, felt the misery surround me, and I accepted it. They wanted to make me feel crazy, I'd be crazy. I had nothing to lose. They weren't going to stop playing with me. She insisted time after time that they were friends. He promised me they would stop talking, then got an app to hide her number.

I hated her because she was so much like me.

She wouldn't quit no matter how hard I tried. He had more trust with his mistress than he did with his wife. She sent me anonymous emails about their being together. I learned how to track IP addresses, and it all led back to her. Still she denied it. I Facebooked her sister, thinking I'd expose their trysts. Her sister told me that I needed to let go and get over the fact that he didn't want me.

What I couldn't accept was that he was playing with my mind. I was losing it over him, and it was one big joke to everyone involved.

You can't ask for directions from people who are lost themselves. Long ago I asked God to order Robert's steps, and now his knee was torn. I didn't blame God, though. I didn't have time to feel His conviction. I wanted *them* to feel my wrath.

We can't avoid God, no matter how hard we try. Even when we think we're getting away, He's still there pulling us. I wasn't going to church. I wasn't watching online. I stopped praying, because I felt my prayers weren't being answered. I still had love for God, but I think a part of me knew I had moved so far out of His will.

I knew I was lost and could no longer find my own way. I just hoped it wasn't too late to be found.

After months of back-and-forth with Robert and his latest con-quest, I was planning to go home. He wasn't playing football due to his injury. Once he completed his rehab, there was no other reason for me to be there. After a trip to Miami, he would come to Texas, too. While he was in Miami, I checked her Facebook page and saw she was there, too. I left for home the same day.

He swore up and down she was stalking him. When he came to Texas, he told my dad he needed an attorney to help get his "stalker" off of him. I rolled my eyes in disbelief. He was willing to do whatever to save face. After a long meeting with my parents about the state of our lives and marriage, we went to bed. The next day I found him playing a video game and texting. I leaned over and looked at his phone. She was six weeks pregnant.

You can't ask for directions from people who are lost themselves.

I had never felt more relieved in my entire life.

After months of trying to make me feel certifiably crazy, my husband's mistress was pregnant! What a long pregnancy it would be.

Once I knew she was pregnant, I think she thought he would leave me, that maybe he just hadn't known how to tell me. But within minutes he was cussing her out, calling her crazy, jealous, a stalker, a groupie, and worse. He turned on her just as quickly as he turned on me. I just sat back and watched it all unfold. I was home and never returning to Virginia again. I didn't care if he stayed or left. I was safe again. I had found a new template for moving forward, the ice trays that would transform my melted self into someone solid again.

So I started the journey of working on me, and me alone. I would decide what to do about Robert later. I went to marital counseling, but for the most part I felt like the other woman's pregnancy had very little to do with me. She had already made it clear that she didn't want me in her child's life, which was fair, because I didn't want her to have a child by my husband. I was doing okay until the sonogram pictures started rolling in. They thought she may be having a girl.

"I don't make anything but girls," he joked with her, finally admitting he might be the father.

I rolled my eyes and thought about the two sons he had lied to me about. When he got upset that she didn't want the baby to have his last name, I enjoyed his strange disappointment. Since they weren't married, her family didn't think it was wise for her to give her child a married man's last name. I knew my parents would've probably felt the same way. Robert was furious. I was, too, for other reasons.

I called Dr. Nicole, our marriage counselor, while sitting in my car. "I'm sorry, but I want them to suffer some consequences," I told her. "I feel like I'm the only one losing here. They've lied, cheated, and tricked around on me for months. She's pregnant and mad at me! He's crying at baby pictures. Where is God in all this?"

Dr. Nicole chastised me for giving Robert and this woman so much power to determine my own well-being. She challenged me to take responsibility for moving forward regardless of what they might be doing, feeling, or baiting me with. She counseled me to express myself to God, trusting Him with my pain, anger, and overwhelming sense of injustice.

I struggled with accepting that they were happy, because I wanted to believe that they would reap what they'd sown. Have you ever wondered when the ones who hurt you were going to pay for what they did? I was bitter because I seemed to be the only one broken in the whole situation. They were discussing the nursery and how we'd split the cost. Yet there was very little focus on his personal responsibility for yet another child he had helped to create. There was no shame between them, as if what they were doing was just part of life, one of those milestones everyone experiences.

Realizing I had to own my own choices, I decided to join their party. Choosing to be bitter doesn't hurt the other person. It only hurts those who come around you. You can't punish them by becoming spiteful and expect God to have any room. Sure, I wasn't ramming cars, but still I let my character suffer because of my attitude. Until you accept that you have no power over when someone will reap what they've sown, you'll always be staring at the ground waiting for their harvest and missing your own.

So I bought hundreds of dollars' worth of clothing and needs for the baby's arrival. I sent her pictures of things I wanted to have framed. I signed the gifts from Makenzie so she would know that I was ready to make her child a part of our family. And every time I felt the temptation to be nasty, I bought something else. I would not let their mistakes determine my happiness.

> *Choosing to be bitter doesn't hurt the other person. It only hurts those who come around you.*

The baby was born two days after my birthday. She didn't want me there, so he didn't go, and that was okay. I was growing stronger.

My friends who knew about the situation took me to dinner. They told me I should start a blog, where I could express the emotion without defining the situation. So I did. I isolated the emotions that I felt and attributed them to someone else's story. Occasionally, I would include one that was genuinely mine. To this day, I've never identified which stories were my own and which were borrowed from someone else's journey. Our pain, disappointment, fear, shame, hope, and desire to live again are all the same.

Robert had his baby, but I had my blog.

I had found this place where it was okay to be broken. Somehow, the words I bled onto the screen reached hearts on the other side, and we became better. I wrote the prayers I whispered myself. I imagined what words could've saved me and put them at the end of each entry.

It would soon be time for Robert to start training camp again. Fresh off his injury, he needed to show that he was healed. But before the movers could even take our things from Texas, Robert was released from the Redskins.

And I blogged.

I blogged about new opportunities. I was glad to say good-bye to the place that had burned me alive. Robert's being released meant I wouldn't have to worry about the woman and her child showing up at our doorstep while my children were sleeping. I returned to work for the ministry. I started traveling and assisting my mom with her book tour. I found a life worth living again.

The more my transparency helped others see themselves in a better light, the more I vowed to tell my truth.

It felt like every time I gave someone the smallest bit of hope, God poured back into me. I used my pain and gave it purpose. I let others know they weren't alone. I talked about the shame, regret, and scorching tears. I was garnering quite the audience, too. No marketing, no gimmicks, just people telling other people about the girl who was willing to keep it so unapologetically real. The more my transparency helped others see themselves in a better light, the more I vowed to tell my truth.

You see, I know what it's like to be drowning. I know what it's like to feel agony. I know what it's like to scan the faces for just one set of eyes that understands your pain.

For me, telling my truth was being that set of eyes.

So what if your past isn't pretty? So what if you gave up more than a few times? You're still here. You have another chance to take your destiny into your hands. Refuse to be ashamed of your truth. It's a part of who you are, helped make you so unbelievably incredible. Scarred? Yes. Wounded? For sure. Afraid? Without a doubt. But you're still here, and that means you can do more than survive. You can live again. You can smile again. And you don't have to be afraid anymore. God doesn't give us the spirit of fear, so if fear is present in your life, it can't be from Him.

While I was on my mother's book tour and meeting people who had read my little blog, I knew I couldn't go back to being that other person. I didn't want a love that made the earth shatter. I wanted a love that made this world better. For some reason, I felt like I could love myself enough to overflow for those still searching.

Having caught wind of my growing audience, the conference staff asked if I would be willing to introduce my dad at our Woman Thou Art Loosed conference. They were only expecting 20,000 women! I didn't want to do it. I was shy. I don't feel like I can speak like a preacher. I'm not even sure that I could say anything that would truly prepare those in attendance for a ministry as dynamic as my father's. But I said yes. I wanted God to know I was willing to stretch myself.

I had stretched so many times for Robert, stretched until I was torn. Surely, I could stretch to be healed.

I thought I had to have Robert at any cost, and he took more than I had to give. I'd give God whatever I had left. Two weeks before Woman Thou Art Loosed, I insisted we get a paternity test for the baby. I'm not sure why at that point I finally demanded something factual and scientific, but it suddenly seemed important. Part of it was just being practical. We had been sending clothes, diapers, and money regularly. It seemed only responsible to know the truth about the paternity.

I was flying home from Chicago when I found out the baby wasn't his. My mother and I shouted all throughout the airport. God was there all along; He just needed me out of the way.

Robert was upset by her betrayal. I didn't even have the time to address the irony of that.

It was over and we were moving on.

That October 2011, I took the stage at Woman Thou Art Loosed, stronger because I had been broken but survived. I gave the last ounce of my pain a voice and talked about how shame had been handcuffing my ability to dream. My father's ministry saved my soul, and I wanted him to know that he hadn't spent his entire life trying to help the world while losing his own daughter.

The message went viral. Women and men alike were applauding me for my courage and commitment to freeing those who didn't have a picture-perfect past. I didn't mean for it to become something so many would see, but that's what happens when you move yourself out of the way. God has more than enough room to blow your mind!

Are you trusting Him with every part of you?

Ironically enough, Robert was in the audience cheering me on. The roles had been reversed, and he would have to stop focusing on his issues long enough to see my gift. People were inviting me to come and share my story all over the world. In February we went to London for my first solo speaking engagement.

Soon I was sharing my story all the time, through my tweets, blogs, speaking engagements, and long hugs with familiar strangers who related to my message. I found a piece of me everywhere I went. And before I knew it, I felt just as strong as people said I was. I didn't feel weak anymore. God's love strengthened me. The support of those yet finding the courage to tell their story encouraged me.

I worked at the church during the day while Robert stayed home at my parents' house playing video games. When I came home from work, he went to play basketball. This was our routine for months and months. In May, I discovered he was playing with more than just video games. The new girl was a student at TCU.

Kenzie was playing on his iPad when the woman's message came through; evidently they were going to meet up while I went to my brother's graduation.

Robert was resting after a long day on the basketball court. I brought the iPad into the room and set it on the nightstand. He knew when he saw my face that things weren't going to end well. I didn't scream, didn't cause a scene; I just asked him to leave.

The thirty-fifth anniversary of my father's ministry was just a couple weeks away. We had been planning a very elaborate celebration, which I didn't want to ruin with the news of another woman. So Robert came back and we attended the celebration. I never treated him any differently. We hugged and smiled for the cameras. Robert thought he was getting another chance. But I knew I was telling him good-bye.

For the last time.

> *I gave the last ounce of my pain a voice and talked about how shame had been handcuffing my ability to dream.*

12

Grace on My Shoulder

AS THIS BOOK reaches bookstores, it will have been almost two years since I made the decision to end my marriage. The culmination of all the things that have happened in my young life have taught me so much about who I am.

I learned to fight. For myself. For the truth. For a love greater than my own need.

I learned that when you have a baby at fourteen, it's hard. Sounds silly, huh? I should've assumed that, but until you've been there, you don't know how hard it is. All I wanted was for people to see my son and me as better. We were more than what the birth certificate and statistic said about us. I became so consumed with planning a better tomorrow for us that I never truly checked to see how everything had truly affected me.

Why did I feel the need to fit in so badly? Why did I need validation from people who were wandering just like me? The fact that

I didn't have a noticeable "church" talent made me more insecure than I wanted to admit.

To this day, one of the first questions people ask me when they find out my father is a pastor is whether I can sing. It's actually amusing, because my singing is terrible. Still, the first thing people want to know is how you fit. I've always used my shyness as an excuse. While that is true to some extent, even if I weren't shy, I wasn't sure what I had to offer.

Having my son made me more defensive. It became my sole mission to protect my son and me. But from what? We weren't in any immediate danger, and even if we were, any threat would have to get past a few dozen people before getting to us. The truth is, I wasn't defensive because of them; I became that way because I was afraid of what came next.

My own insecurity affected how I thought the world would view me. I called myself every name in the book, just so that I could get used to hearing them. Everything from a ho to a black sheep, I tried to train myself to take the abuse.

I thought that beating others to the punch would lessen the blow. I cried for my son. He was so beautiful and innocent, born to someone who didn't know if she could give him the life he deserved. I didn't give myself permission to not have the answers. By college, when my rush to recover started failing, I didn't retreat or lighten my load. I quit. I gave up and tried to create a new plan.

I attracted insecurity to myself. It comforted me until it broke me.

That is when my life came to a fork in the road. Would I be willing to let an insecurity haunt me for the rest of my life?

Like me, you will have to decide how you let your insecurities affect you. Will you settle for heartbreak because you've already been broken? No matter how many times I tried to adjust to a life of recurring pain, I heard this whisper inside of me insisting there was more. I tried countless times to drown the sound of that voice in my head, but I couldn't. It was with me at the end of every night and the beginning of each day: *"God, please help me."*

After my divorce, I ran across an anonymous quote online that spoke to my wounded heart and has stayed with me: "No matter what, once in your life, someone will hurt you. That someone will take all that you are and rip it into pieces, and they won't even watch where the pieces land. But through the breakdown, you'll learn something about yourself. You'll learn that you're strong and, no matter how hard they try to destroy you, you can conquer anyone."

Even yourself, I would add.

I stayed in my marriage until I felt like leaving wouldn't break me. There was a part of me holding on to the treatment because I felt like it was all I deserved. When that was no longer the case, it became about my children. Maybe I could learn to turn this into an agreement where Robert and I only stayed together for them. I didn't want to hurt both of my children by upsetting their lives just because I was bleeding.

When you love your children, really love them, their hearts come before your own. If I couldn't have my fairy tale, at least I could try to give them one. We would look like the perfect little family, and I would learn to deal with the pain for them.

There's this thing about family that I should've remembered from

> *You will have to decide how you let your insecurities affect you. Will you settle for heartbreak because you've already been broken?*

when my stomach started growing with life the first time. When one bleeds, we all bleed. I was bleeding on them and didn't know it. Children have the most accurate radar of happiness. I thought I was making them happy. I didn't realize that my own happiness ultimately set the tone.

My mother had asked me to start working for the ministry before I knew about the first affair. The moment I started working, I gained back a little bit of myself. It wasn't the money or having something to do, either. It was that I was learning that I could still be used.

In the end, the ministry I tried to outrun most of my life is what saved me. I wasn't sure if the team of ladies my mother trusted me to support, organize, and lead would respect me. I brought my heart for my mother and the need to create something beautiful to the women's ministry of our church. Each day, I went to the place where I first felt like an outcast and carved a space for me.

Every other Saturday, a group of women gathered in the main sanctuary of our church for our life-enrichment program. The ages for the course ranged from eighteen to ninety years old. Together we all had one desire: We wanted to believe that life still had something great for us. My first year helping my mother with the ministry, I did everything from the background—booking the speakers, creating the schedule, managing the budget, creating exercises to help stretch the ladies, and more. As long as I didn't have to make any announcements or do anything that brought attention to myself, I was fine.

No one knew how bad my marriage was, and in the safety of those walls it didn't matter. All that mattered was that each Saturday I gave the women in our church a Christ-centered program that would make them better. I wanted the girls in our debutante program to avoid the insecurities that left me trapped.

For the women, I wanted them to take a chance on themselves. Then I wondered what I was waiting for. My blog was my taking a chance on myself. It was my daring to believe in the message I was orchestrating for them. When my first class graduated from the program, I cried because I was proud of them. I cried because I was one of them.

I truly can't say that I ended my marriage because of the cheating, the lies, or the betrayal. The moment it hit me that I would never be able to accept a counterfeit of real love, I knew our relationship had a countdown.

I wanted to turn the other cheek and pretend that it didn't hurt. I had tried everything to make it better. I got angry. I lost my mind. I went to counseling. I left. I cried. I cussed. I never mastered the art of accepting it, though. I felt like I was weak, but there was a part of me that I evidently had no control over. That part of me wasn't willing to lie down and die.

A week before my eighteenth birthday, Robert and I had gotten tattoos. I never thought about getting one before then. But I didn't want him to think I wasn't down to have fun. I tried to pick something that I wouldn't regret in three weeks. I settled on a Chinese symbol on my right shoulder. "What does it mean?" Robert asked me when I sat down.

"Grace," I said.

Once the tattoo healed, I honestly forgot it was there. I got it before I knew how badly I would need it. All along when I felt the most alone, grace was still with me. When I was ramming cars and fighting to be free, grace was right there on my shoulder. When I cried for the little girl I lost along the way, grace was under my skin. I didn't even realize, until I took the time to write this book and tell you about finding my way, just how much grace was with me all along. Grace is not the absence of the struggle; it is the presence of protection.

My life hasn't been perfect at all. This isn't a fairy tale, but it is a story of restoration and amazing grace. I constantly tried to give grace in my marriage, but I was unable to accept the grace that God was giving me. The moment I started to tap into that grace, I became better.

Grace is not the absence of the struggle; it is the presence of protection.

He gave me the grace to protect my children even in the midst of a hurricane love affair. God gave me the grace to avoid completely losing myself to a crime of passion or life-threatening disease. I found the grace to admit that I needed to come home. All along, right there on my shoulder, out of sight but with me all the time was grace.

When will you trust that you've got the grace to go past survival and collide with destiny? Are you willing to believe that grace rests on your shoulders as well?

I didn't know if my heart could be mended. I didn't know if my future could be restored. I'm not even sure I felt redemption was possible, but I trusted grace wouldn't leave me just because my marriage was over. Not even six months after my divorce was final, I sat outside on the patio of the home grace helped me purchase. I needed to go inside so that I could write the book you're reading right now, but I stayed a little longer and that's when I saw the Big Dipper. Just like grace, it's been there waiting for me to recognize it.

The result of all these beautiful, tragic moments in my life once made me so hungry for forgiveness. But they were never meant to make me feel like I was less than; they were meant to show me His

One detour

doesn't cancel

our destination.

grace. We try to make our mistakes about *us*, but maybe God wants to know if we can give Him every part of us.

We don't get to determine which pieces of us He can use. Though He can and will use what we give Him, His strength is made perfect when we give Him our weakness. At Woman Thou Art Loosed, I gave Him the last drop of shame from my pregnancy. I no longer wanted to be bound. I told my father I wanted to tell the world before the world tried to use it against me. For me, divorce wasn't about trying to teach Robert a lesson; it was me choosing me. I always felt the most weak when I was with him. I had trusted him with my insecurity, but then I gave it to God.

I learned too much about myself to continue to accept punishment for a crime that had been washed with the blood of Christ.

Accepting my imperfections and God's undeniable love for me has been the most life-changing thing I've ever experienced. I wasn't afraid to let Him have His way; I just doubted that I could be of use to Him. I'm not telling my story so it can be criticized, though I know it will be. A part of me is afraid to let the world know even a fraction of what I shared. The more I meet people and remember my own lost moments, the more I truly believe that the message is more important than my shame, my ego, or their criticism.

This is for you. For me. For us.

This is a reminder that one detour doesn't cancel our destination. These words are for the whispers that haunt us and tell us life is over. This book is for your shattered pieces.

You have been beautifully wounded.

As I shared earlier, a few months before my twenty-fifth birthday, I learned that my father was going to Australia for the Hillsong Conference right around my birthday. I begged him to let me go with him and experience the friendly people and natural beauty of

Down Under as well as the powerful worship and teaching at the conference. My first night in attendance, the worship leader led us in a song so powerful, I didn't even have to write it down to remember it: "Glorious Ruins."

What an oxymoron!

How can something that's been ruined be glorious? Then I looked at my life and remembered when I was most devastated, and how now at twenty-five, I had inspired thousands of people. Could it be that our sin is not in being ruined, but in not letting Him find the glory in our pieces?

I don't know what your story is, but I gave you the worst parts of mine so that you could know that someone else hit rock bottom, too. You're not alone. We are not alone. We have to embrace these ugly truths about ourselves, or we'll spend a lifetime never maximizing the ever-present grace surrounding us.

Could it be that our sin is not in being ruined, but in not letting Him find the glory in our pieces?

Each day, I wake up feeling like I'm living a dream. I didn't know that happiness like this could exist. I still have hard days. My relationships with people still go through tremendous ups and downs. My life isn't perfect by any means, but it has been kissed by grace and I am surrounded by joy.

I don't know if you're lost right now or finding your way. But if the sun rises tomorrow, you have a chance to test the limits of God's grace. He's capable of making you better. He can take every moment you thought was wasted and use it to create a story that helps someone else believe. You have to try to trust Him with the parts of you that still hurt. He's not expecting perfection.

All He needs is a yes.

And not a yes that is contingent on whether or not He does what you want. It wasn't that I was never going to say yes to Him, because I honestly think I would have found my way back. I just wanted to present a perfect life for Him to use. He just wanted *me*. God gave me the desires of my heart, and then He gave me what He desired for me. His plan was much better than my own.

> *I just wanted to present a perfect life for Him to use. He just wanted me.*

If you aren't careful, you'll let your past talk you out of your destiny.

I don't know what's next for me. This could be the last book I ever write, or it could be the beginning of something huge, but I'm not afraid. And maybe I had to live with fear for so long that it lost its bite, because now I feel like I can do anything with God on my side.

So can you.

Conclusion

Being Found

AT THE BEGINNING of this book, I shared with you how frequently my kids' forgotten jackets and misplaced backpacks send me to their school's collection of lost and found items. What strikes me during these visits is that these things are both simultaneously lost *and* found. When we lose something, we only think of it as missing, absent, perhaps gone forever. But often these same things are what someone else finds and wonders about. They want to know where the item came from, whom it belongs to, and where to return it.

So often in our lives, we dwell on our lostness without remembering that God has already found us and wants to help us locate our destiny. In those times when the road is dark, the night is long, and the storm rages with unrelenting fury; when we can barely see the next step in front of our eyes, let alone the correct route to our original destination—we know we're lost, disoriented, uncertain, and afraid. We don't know where we are or how we'll ever get to where we want to go.

Until we find ourselves.

It's a funny expression, "finding ourselves." I hear people say, "And then before I knew it, I found myself driving to the mall"—or wherever—as if they had lost awareness of themselves and their decisions before coming back and realizing where they were and what they were doing. But I think we all feel that way sometimes. Like the prodigal son coming to his senses, awakened by the stench of his own bad decisions, we find ourselves and realize where we are is not where we belong.

Then we remember the way home.

The chapters of my life I've shared with you within these pages reveal some of my darkest hours and most painful disappointments. But as a broken window acts as a prism, filtering sunlight through its cracks, I hope that you can see the many beautiful moments of color dancing within my rooms. My children bring me so much joy that sometimes I just shake my head at their antics and laugh, and then, when they're not looking, allow the tears to well up as my heart floods with so much love for them.

More and more, I find myself looking up with newfound clarity at the Big Dipper and other constellations. I see the North Star glinting like a lighthouse made of diamonds and know I've found myself. I feel the wind caress my face and smell piñon and cottonwood on the Texas breeze, and my spirit overflows. Sitting in my house, the one I've worked so hard to purchase and furnish and infuse with love for my children, I cherish the moments when I can just relax and know that I am home.

When I speak in front of thousands of people, still nervous in my body but confident in my soul of what I have to say, I feel God holding me close to Him. I feel so grateful that sharing my story might help others. He was there all along, even those times when I kept ignoring the whisper of His voice or the detours from my pain He

With stubborn determination

to see only what we want to see,

we walk along a treacherous

path until we finally fall off the

cliff of pride and land on the

humility of our neediness.

provided. I never quit believing in Him, but I found it hard to believe that He could continue to care about me after all I had done. Surely He was just as disappointed in my decisions as my parents were at times. Surely He judged me with an even harsher standard than the one I used to constantly punish myself. Surely He wanted me to prove myself worthy of his love and attention the way Robert did.

Only He doesn't. A large part of being found comes from surrendering your pride and accepting God's grace. When your car breaks down and you're stranded on the side of the road, would you refuse the assistance of a tow truck that stops to rescue you? Why, then, do we so often try to push the car ourselves (uphill!) when God offers to rebuild our engine?

I don't believe we can lose our salvation. Once we have committed to Christ and experienced the grace of God, we are always found. But we do lose ourselves and lose sight of the divine destiny that God wants to reveal to us. With stubborn determination to see only what we want to see, we walk along a treacherous path until we finally fall off the cliff of pride and land on the humility of our neediness.

God always picks us up and reminds us that He has more for us. More than we can imagine. More than we can see from where we've fallen.

Of all the people who helped me during the crazy twists and turns my young life has taken so far, there's one that I have never met in person. She's a young woman, probably not unlike me, a minority in the society in which she ultimately found herself. She, too, had lost a husband, although it was his death that left her single and not the death of their marriage. She had nothing but was willing to do what it took to survive, even eating the leftovers she could find after others had finished. Although she didn't have children to take care of yet, she was devoted to the care of her beloved mother-in-law.

If you've read my book *Colliding With Destiny*, then you know I'm talking about Ruth (and if you haven't read it, you should!). This amazing woman knew what it meant to lose her dream, her homeland, and her hopes for the future. She could justifiably have remained at home in Moab instead of following Naomi back to Bethlehem. Based on the terrible turn of events in her life, she could've played the victim card and no one would've faulted her. Or she could've become bitter, like her mother-in-law.

But Ruth ventured forward with a personal resolve and a fledgling faith in the God that she had only recently met. I'm sure there must have been times when she wondered if she could really trust Him with her future. Or maybe she worried that He really didn't care about the details of her life. But she didn't give up.

Ruth knew that while she often felt lost, she was already found. God had found her, and she only had to catch up to Him. She was on a trajectory for triumph despite the trials that were her launching pad. When she was lonely and afraid, uncertain and confused, angry and aching, Ruth could not see the joy that was around the bend. When the cupboard echoed with emptiness almost as loud as her stomach, Ruth couldn't imagine that she would soon find grain waiting on the ground. She could not yet see the loving husband, Boaz, and their baby son waiting up ahead of her.

Through it all Ruth kept going.

I believe she knew the secret to being found: Never give up your hope. Keep the embers of hope alive as best you can, even when the wind reduces it to a handful of sparks. Don't allow the tears to fill your eyes to the point that you can't see the grain on the ground in front of you. Don't doubt the abundant, blessed grace of a Father who loves you as His precious child, who wants more for you than you can even imagine for yourself.

So much of the biblical truth that I heard as a child probably went in one ear and out the other. But some of those seeds took root. And for me, Ruth has been a gardener of those seeds of truth in my soul. She reminds me that when the worst happens, it will get better. Even when we can't imagine being happy again, we will.

Jesus said, "For whoever wants to save their life will lose it, but whoever loses their life for me will find it" (Matthew 16:25). Sometimes we have to let go of where we think we're going in order to discover where we're meant to be. God shows us the way if we let Him. No matter how lost you think you are, or how many times you've been found and wandered off again, it's never too late to be found again. We're all lost and found.

And I'm living proof of that.

SARAH JAKES is a businesswoman, writer, speaker, and media personality. She oversees the women's ministry at The Potter's House of Dallas, a multicultural, nondenominational church and humanitarian organization led by her parents, Bishop T.D. Jakes and Mrs. Serita Jakes.

In addition to her duties at The Potter's House, Sarah is the senior editor of the online magazine *eMotions*, which is designed to educate and empower women. She also periodically serves as host of *The Potter's Touch*, a daily inspirational broadcast airing on several national television networks. With her husband, Touré Roberts, she ministers to those in the TV, film, and music industries.

Sarah blogs on love, life, family, and marriage and aspires to write articles and books that chronicle the lives of young women who have overcome extreme challenges to reach their goals in life. In addition to sharing her personal journey in *Lost and Found*, Sarah offers encouragement for women in *Colliding With Destiny*.

When she is not pursuing her career endeavors, Sarah enjoys cooking, listening to music, and spending quality time with her husband and children. They make their home in the Los Angeles area. Connect with her online at sarahjakes.com.